A Championship Coach's Formula for
Achieving Breakthrough Results

GET MORE

FOR COACHES

Empower Your Athletes to Do More, Be More, and
GET MOR^{3}EE Out of Their Talents and Potential

JOBY SLAY, MBA

GET MORE FOR COACHES
Copyright ©2020 Joby Slay
All rights reserved
International Standard Book Number 978-1-988928-23-4 soft cover
ISBN 978-1-988928-24-1 EPUB

Published by: Castle Quay Books
Burlington, ON, Canada | Riviera Beach, FL, USA
Tel: (416) 573-3249
E-mail: info@castlequaybooks.com | www.castlequaybooks.com

Edited by Marina Hofman Willard
Book cover and interior by Burst Impressions

Library and Archives Canada Cataloguing in Publication

Title: Get more for coaches : a championship coach's formula for achieving breakthrough results /
  Joby Slay.
Names: Slay, Joby, author.
Identifiers: Canadiana 2019020107X | ISBN 9781988928234 (softcover)
Subjects: LCSH: Coaching (Athletics) | LCSH: Motivation (Psychology) | LCSH: Achievement motivation.
Classification: LCC GV711 .S63 2019 | DDC 796.07/7—dc23

CASTLE QUAY BOOKS

This book is dedicated to all the coaches who serve our communities and earnestly desire to help our youth of today and tomorrow get more out of their talent and potential. Your modeling of servant leadership and commitment to excellence will exponentially multiply the success of our tomorrows.

To Papa, the greatest coach I've ever known, and Gran, the coach's wife. Thank you for leaving it all on the field for us and leaving an undying legacy by modeling integrity, honesty, and teaching. Thank you for serving and leading in the community, gifting compassion and coaching love.

"Coach Joby Slay's book unpacks the philosophy and practical applications of how to become leaders who get more out of themselves and the people they are responsible to influence. I've studied the science of coaching for twenty years at the highest levels and have watched Coach Slay implement his GET MORE ideas for multiple seasons, and the results speak for themselves. His teams steadily improve and have fulfilling experiences filled with lessons they will take with them beyond athletics. I'd recommend this book to any leader in any context but especially sport coaches."

Dr. Chris Hobbs
Varsity Brands National Athletic Director of the Year, 2019
Coach & A.D. Magazine 40 Under 40 sports leader

"*GET MORE FOR COACHES*, written by Joby Slay, lays out a logical and uncomplicated approach for coaches to implement in their coaching style that goes beyond just developing a successful team. The book goes beyond coaching philosophy by introducing concepts along with examples that are easily adapted to a coach's own approach and are sure to raise the coaches' impact on the kids they coach, both on and off the field. The unexpected and beautiful value I found in Joby's coaching philosophy is the combination of simple concepts that exponentially increase the impact that each concept in the GET MOR^{3}EE formula has alone.

"Joby's ability to combine the concepts, formula, and personal stories makes it extremely easy for me to take away actionable improvements to my own process when coaching kids. The book has a great combination of education, motivation, and humor. I recommend coaches and parents alike to read the book. For those who do read it, I am positive that the readers will take notes, as I found myself doing when reading *GET MORE FOR COACHES* and the GET MOR^{3}EE formula."

Andrew Mehalko, CFA
Partner, co-chief investment officer
Forbes Family Trust
3x NCAA Men's Soccer National Champion, All-American and NCAA
Tournament MVP, UNC-Greensboro

"Joby is an amazing husband, father, friend, and coach! Now, he gets to add amazing author to that list! Kids love playing for him, and parents are looking for opportunities for their children to play for him. My daughter was lucky enough to be on his team in recreation soccer a few years ago and had a great experience. She wasn't the best player, but Joby helped her find her strengths, and she grew tremendously. I've been coaching middle school sports for a number of years and have led some of my teams to championships in soccer and flag football. However, after reading an early draft of Joby's book *GET MORE FOR COACHES*, I'm going to be able to take my coaching to an even higher level."

Jon Payne
Athletic administrator and coach

"Joby is the real deal! It comes from his heart, and I have seen him coach many different types of people, some harder to coach than others, but he eventually reaches them all with genuine connection, patience, and kindness. It's so important to have a coach/mentor who believes in himself and also in those he helps. He gives 110 percent of himself, and I am sure he has completely changed some children's lives for the better!"

Eliza Stephenson Meyer
Parent of former youth player

CONTENTS

COACHING PLAN:
A WORD FOR THE READER

The entire goal of this project is to share with coaches and readers the simple acronym that I've used in my everyday leadership and coaching for the past 15 years. The GET MOR³EE acronym was created for me to easily recall what I observed and experienced as the most important principles of successful leadership and coaching.

Over 15 years of filtering my coaching decisions through the lens of this acronym led to the development of the GET MOR³EE formula. The success I've experienced with my players and teams I contribute largely to the consistent application of the GET MOR³EE formula. The formula is simple but effective, and the results are powerful. This tool has benefited me in business and coaching to lead, encourage, and empower the people under my influence. I describe the formula in detail and explain how you can easily implement it in your coaching. I promise it will enhance the way you lead and coach, resulting in positive breakthroughs with your players and team.

The "GET MOR³EE Coach" chapter supplements the GET MOR³EE formula by describing many of the qualities displayed by coaches who have the ultimate desire to help their players get more out of their talent and potential.

It's most important that you as a coach are able to recall the GET MOR³EE acronym. Study it. Learn it. Internalize the GET MOR³EE formula for your coaching and leading. Take a picture of the cycle so you can pull it up on your cell phone before training sessions or when facing a difficult decision with a player. Use it as a lens to filter your coaching decisions. Apply it in your coaching program, tailor it to your personality, and allow it to enhance your coaching.

Scattered throughout this book you will find little side notes titled "Coaches' Box." The Coaches' Boxes are additional thoughts and ideas that I think will be helpful for you but are not necessary pieces of the GET MOR^{3}EE formula. Just another coaching idea, tip, or practical application from my coaching experience and observations.

At the end of each chapter is a scouting report. The scouting report is a bullet point reminder of the important quotes, ideas, and thoughts from the chapter. I use stories and analogies in each chapter to help connect the reader to these points. Some readers may want to hit the scouting report first or quickly refer back to it in the future.

CHAPTER 1
THE COACH'S POTENTIAL

I imagine a world where the greatest harvest of the 21st century will be the harvest of human potential.

THE NFL DRAFT

Once a year, usually around the end of April, millions of people gather around their televisions, tablets, and cell phones to devour the NFL draft. Months of research, millions of dollars, and countless hours of study and analysis go into evaluating and rating a few thousand college football players in their early 20s. What is being evaluated? Human potential. Specifically, the potential to play football at the professional level. Why is it so important? Why is so much time and money invested? Because the decision of which young man a front office picks to play for its football team is the difference between winning and losing. It may be the difference in a coach's or general manager's career.

Why is our culture so fascinated in watching a broadcast of television personalities discussing why or where a player should be drafted? Why are football fanatics so infatuated that they pore over draft grades on scouting and news websites? Because in our society we are constantly evaluating and putting grades on people's value and potential. We watch the NFL draft and cheer or boo our team's draft picks based on whether we believe the team got value in its pick. If Tom Brady had been drafted in the first round, the fans would have booed because no team believed he had that type of potential. In the late rounds, no one cared. The challenge with evaluating human potential is that none of us can predict the future. The person with the best idea of what a player may become is inside that player. The rest of us are reduced to trying to predict a player's future based upon past performances. The challenge with trying to predict the potential of Tom Brady was that he wasn't even a full-time starter at the University of Michigan. The majority of people thought Michigan's other quarterback, Drew Henson, had more potential. Brady's coach at Michigan didn't seem to be fully confident in Brady's ability. When analyzing Tom Brady through those circumstances, it would have been hard for anyone to believe he would ever win six Super Bowls, but two short years later, he quarterbacked the New England Patriots in his first Super Bowl win.

As coaches, the majority of the time we have to make decisions based on current and recent performances. We can tend to overvalue great performances **and** overvalue poor performances. What do I mean? If a player first has a great performance in our presence, then we tend to remember that great performance, and we grade the potential of that player based on that great performance. Rightly or wrongly, we may invest more in that player when he or she struggles because we believe the player can perform better and has a higher potential, based on witnessing a great performance. Conversely, if we first witness a poor performance by a player, we may now evaluate that player's future potential based on that first performance. We are later surprised if the player performs better. None of us can predict the future. Especially when it comes to people. We can make highly informed guesstimations, but we can't put a lid on a person's potential. There are too many variables and too much time and opportunities for people to know where they will end up.

This is why the GET MOR³EE formula is such a good resource for coaches. It helps us to manage our own tendencies to rate players on past performances and to continue to build and invest into all the players under our charge regardless of how we perceive their physical performances. We have the challenge of managing the short-term results of our teams with the long-term development of the individuals. The GET MOR³EE formula is our guide for accomplishing both challenges as coaches. It's the formula for empowering our players and maximizing their potential.

"What lies behind us and what lies before us are tiny matters compared to what lies within us." (Attributed to Henry S. Haskins)

WHAT IS POTENTIAL?

How can we know if a person or team has maximized their potential? I think it's important to put a timeframe on that question. "Potential" by definition is an ability or capacity to be or develop into something in the future. Our potential abilities in a year are different than what they may be in five years. With sports, I think it's simple. How do we know if we've maximized our potential as individual athletes and as a team by the end of a season? I think there are two parts to the answer. One: when players can unabashedly tell me they've given every last drop of commitment, effort, and focus to fulfill their potential in this area and put their potential into action. And two: when I as their coach confirm that to be true. Then I can say that a player has maximized his or her potential in that moment.

It's one thing to **reach** your potential. It's another thing to **fulfill** your potential and another to **maximize** your potential.

Reaching your potential is a discovery process. It requires learning and growing. You've arrived at your potential. You've discovered a talent and seen a glimpse of what you could do with that talent. There is a spark.

Fulfilling your potential requires aligning your potential talent with a purpose. Your purpose can be as simple as a goal you set for the season. The thought of your talent and purpose together brings you joy and excitement. It brings you focus and clarity. There is energy. There is motivation. Maximizing your potential requires putting your talent and purpose into action. Maximizing your potential enlarges the influence of your talent and purpose. There is movement. There is momentum.

I believe it to be an honor and a responsibility as a coach to help players discover, fulfill, and maximize their talents and potential.

How do you know if a kid has more potential? They're breathing.

"Much of leadership is about extracting the extra 5 per cent of performance that individuals did not know they possessed." (Sir Alex Ferguson)[1]

---

1. Alex Ferguson and Michael Moritz, *Leading* (New York: Hachette Books, 2015), 47.

GET MOR³EE'S RELEVANCE AND OPPORTUNITY IN TODAY'S COACHING ENVIRONMENT

I am a coach, and I grew up as the grandson of a hall of fame coach who left an echoing legacy. The most influential people in my life have all been coaches. The foundation of many of the ideas and observations of GET MOR³EE came from observing and studying coaches and teams in competition over a season or seasons—much of it at the youth level.

We now face the challenge of a technological society where technology has both brought us closer together and at the same time drawn us farther apart. We have the ability to communicate more easily than ever before, but we struggle to keep the focus of our youth with so many things competing for their attention. How do we help them stay on task when it's so easy to move on to the next thing when they face adversity? How do we still challenge them to strive for a goal and achieve more than they maybe thought possible?

In a world where social media influencers are all the rage, have we forgotten about the most powerful influencer in a person's life? The coach. The coach is still one of the greatest influencers and most impactful people in an adolescent's life. The coach has the opportunity to have the undivided attention of a youth for an hour or two at a time, several times a week, and without the distractions of tablets and technology. Their parents may not even get that much connected time.

It has become obvious to me that I must share my leadership and coaching philosophy on how to grow and develop the people in your charge and get more out of them. Coaches are attracted to the easy-to-apply formula for motivating their players to achieve more. We need to be able to inspire and equip coaches to coach the **person** and not just the player. We need to empower athletes to increase the positivity in their environment and eliminate the "trash" talk that has become so prevalent and accepted in our youth athletics today. An appropriate proverb from the wisest man that ever lived is "Good people bless and build up their city, but the wicked can destroy it with their words" (Prov. 11:11 NCV).

MY FOCUS

My focus has never been on winning every game. My heart has always been on winning with every player. That doesn't mean getting them to like me. My role is not to be their friend, but I can be friendly. My role is to be their coach. A teacher, leader, mentor, and cheerleader all rolled into one. My number one responsibility is to motivate the players to succeed at whatever we define success to be—to be one of their biggest cheerleaders and supporters, while also holding them accountable to themselves and the team. How you do that depends on you as the coach and where you're going, but I have a formula you can follow that's helped me in guiding teams in countless winning seasons and countless winning people. I developed the formula by observing my grandfather, a hall of fame coach, and observing and studying other successful and unsuccessful coaches and leaders.

Most recently, I implemented the formula over the past three years with the varsity boys' soccer team at The Kings Academy. When I took over in 2016, we started our rise by defeating two teams in our district that we never beat in the history of our school. The two coaches both approached me afterwards to congratulate me—not necessarily on the win but on how different the team looked, how confident and motivated the boys seemed compared to previous years. We made it to the district final, and one of those coaches, whose team we beat again in the playoffs, told me he was voting for me for Coach of the Year.

I was not selected as Coach of the Year that year, but I thought it was cool that other coaches validated the work we were doing in a year when we didn't win the championship. The following season of 2017, we were in the district final again, only losing one district game all season to the team that eventually won the state championship. In the 2018/19 season we started the season 2–7–1, but I just knew we were going to win the district. I kept instilling that belief in the boys, even when at our lowest. We finished the season on a 6–0 run through the playoffs, conceding just one goal. Our team defeated the reigning state champions, finally winning the district championship in 2019 for only the third time in school history. We then advanced through the first round of the regional playoffs for only the second time in school history. I was voted Coach of the Year in 2019 after winning the district championship, which was satisfying, and I was appreciative of all the coaches who voted for me.

I walked into a team of high school boys with very few full-time soccer players, who were struggling to compete in the conference and low on confidence. Transforming them into a group that believed they could compete successfully, reaching the district finals all three seasons, and winning the district championship in 2019 didn't occur by happenstance. I was purposeful in following the GET MOR³EE formula. My goal was to get to the district championship every season.

I started with a bold vision of getting to the last game, the state championship. Then I focused on developing the players. We can't be certain of what the ultimate outcome will be at the end of the season. We focus on getting more out of each player. My ultimate goal and measure of success is whether I am able to get the most out of every player. Maybe, maybe not, because I believe there is more yet to come, but maybe we did in that season. The success is that we got more out of some of our players than some of them imagined possible.

THE GREATEST CHALLENGE IN YOUTH SPORTS

It may be that the most significant challenge facing youth sports today is the lack of sufficiently trained athletic coaches. The Aspen Institute has studied this extensively and reports, "Coaches are the delivery mechanism for quality sport programming ... They can make an athlete for life—or wreck enthusiasm for sport altogether ... Trained coaches do best."[2] However, "Less than four in 10 youth coaches say they are trained in any of the following areas: sport skills and tactics, effective motivational technique, or safety needs (CPR/basic first aid and concussion management)."[3]

Effective motivational techniques and sports skills/tactics are the skill sets we most often associate with good coaching. According to this study, only 36 percent of coaches have received training in effective motivational techniques and 35 percent in sports skills/tactics. The Aspen Institute report provides this information:

2. "State of Play 2018: Trends and Developments," The Aspen Institute, 14, accessed October 7, 2019, https://assets.aspeninstitute.org/content/uploads/2018/10/StateofPlay2018_v4WEB_2-FINAL.pdf?_ga=2.20463032.149414129.1569891254-1271466118.1569891254.
3. Jon Solomon and Tom Farrey, "10 Charts that Show Progress, Challenges to Fix Youth Sports," The Aspen Institute (October 16, 2018), https://www.aspeninstitute.org/blog-posts/10-charts-that-show-progress-challenges-to-fix-youth-sports/.

YOUTH COACHES WITH TRAINING
Percentage of 2017 coaches who say they received specified training

39% CPR/BASIC FIRST AID

36% GENERAL SAFETY AND INJURY PREVENTION

36% EFFECTIVE MOTIVATIONAL TECHNIQUES

35% SPORTS SKILLS AND TACTICS*

31% PHYSICAL CONDITIONING

29% CONCUSSION MANAGEMENT

In primary sport they coach

Here is why the skill of effective motivation may be the most important in improving youth sports in America. A youth sports study on why students quit a sports team showed that 39 percent of students responded that they weren't having fun.[4] This is an alarming figure and was by far the biggest reason statistically of why students quit playing. At the core, I believe this is a function of the environment created by the coach. Following the GET MOR³EE formula equips coaches to begin building this environment.

The following is an excerpt from an April 10, 2019, Stack.com post titled "A Shocking Number of Youth Sports Coaches Are Unqualified for the Gig."

A 2004 report from the University of Maine found that youth athletes who play for an untrained coach drop at a rate of 26% per year, while those who play for a qualified coach drop out at 5%. The NAYS states that kids and pre-teens are more likely to experience a boost in self-esteem when playing for a qualified coach as opposed to an unqualified coach. Qualified coaches know how to make practices fun, safe and age-appropriate …

According to research by the Aspen Institute's Project Play initiative, kids want coaches who:

• Respect and encourage them
• Exist as positive role models
• Offer clear, consistent communication

---

4. Don Sabo and Phil Veliz, "Go Out and Play: Youth Sports in America," Women's Sports Foundation (October, 2008), 130, https://files.eric.ed.gov/fulltext/ED539976.pdf.

- Have a knowledge of the sport
- Have a willingness to listen.[5]

Knowledge of the sport is just one of the top five traits that players hope for in a coach. The other four are relational by nature—traits of a mentor, teacher, and coach.

"Coaches can often be more helpful to a young player's development by organizing less, saying less, and allowing the players to do more."[6] As coaches we need to create an environment that naturally empowers and encourages players to do more. An empowered player gains the self-confidence to take initiative in doing more, which fuels their creativity, imagination, and passion and creates even greater momentum and motivation.

Youth sports is such a large demographic that no one really knows how many kids are participating annually, but I've seen figures estimating that somewhere between 30 to 45 million kids annually participate in organized youth sports in America alone.

If each kid participated in just one organized sport annually, then the preceding number means there will be possibly 300 to 450 million opportunities over the next decade for a coach to positively impact a child during a season of youth sports. This is a generational opportunity, but let us put aside the number of kids for a moment and focus on what may be the more important figure.

An estimated 3.5 million youth coaches in America are coaching these 30 to 45 million kids a year. That averages out to about 1 coach for every 10 kids participating in organized sports, and this number may not accurately reflect the millions of part-time parent coaches. According to the Stack.com article, the larger challenge facing youth sports is finding qualified coaches. If only 36 percent of 3.5 million coaches have training in effective motivational techniques, then roughly 2.25 million coaches have a need for a practical tool like the GET MOR³EE formula. If the NAYS

5. *Best Practices for Coaching Soccer in the United States*, quoted in Brandon Hall, "A Shocking Number of Youth Sports Coaches Are Unqualified for the Gig," Stack.com (April 10, 2019), https://www.stack.com/a/a-shocking-number-of-youth-sports-coaches-are-unqualified-for-the-gig.
6. "Player Development Guidelines: Best Practices for Coaching Soccer in the United States," United States Soccer Federation, accessed September 30, 2019, http://www.pghdynamo.org/doclib/090903_Best_Practicespdf.pdf.

GET MORE FOR COACHES

estimate of only 5 to 10 percent of youth coaches having any relevant training is anywhere close to accurate, then there is a **massive need** to meet.

Whenever I hear a story from parents or coaches about a coach's poor behavior or seeming lack of coaching ability, I ask them why they think that is the case. The majority of the responses include a reference to the coach as "unequipped." Unequipped is exactly what the Alpine Group study describes. Equipping coaches is the greatest value of the GET MOR^{3}EE formula. There is a clear need to equip coaches with a simple motivational tool to apply in coaching their players and teams. If we can do that, I think we will begin to have fewer complaints about the lack of coaching ability. If we do hear "unequipped" associated with the description of a coach's ability to lead and motivate, then instead of being constantly frustrated, we have a way to encourage and equip more coaches, not just to be more positive but also to be empowering leaders and role models for our youth.

CHAPTER TWO
THE GET MOR³EE FORMULA

The GET MOR³EE formula for coaches is so simple to teach and apply. This book organizes the many principles of winning motivational coaching into a simple-to-recall formula for applying in your teams. Whether you are a new coach or a 30-year veteran, the GET MOR³EE formula for motivating and encouraging your teams to higher achievement will improve your coaching acumen. GET MOR³EE is an acronym for the properties that compose the formula I'm sharing with you.

In this chapter I summarize the seven properties that make up the GET MOR³EE formula for you. The properties mentioned more than likely won't be anything you haven't heard before. You may even practice some application of these properties already in your coaching. They are all components of effective leadership and coaching. I simply organized the properties into an easy-to-recall system and formula for practical application with my teams.

Don't get hung up on the ordering of the properties too much. I do think the acronym helps as a reminder to think about them in this order, but I believe that as long as you are making sure to connect and touch on each of these properties with your team, you will have success. **Motivation** and **ownership** are definitely more foundational, so I like to start with establishing the foundation of those components with my players and team. I try to convey the concept of ownership early with my teams, as the **R³** properties are best enhanced and understood through the concept of ownership. **Encouragement** can and should be sprinkled around anywhere and everywhere. You may even begin the relationship by encouraging a person, and that is what brings them into a relationship with you.

Encouragement is effective anywhere. **Empowerment** is the product we are seeking as a result of mixing together the other properties fully.

Developing your understanding and building your coaching acumen in any one of the properties will help you develop as a coach, but learning how to mix them all together and why will equip you to take your players and your team to heights that you and they didn't know they could go. Whether you are a new coach or 20-year veteran, I applaud you for being curious and seeking additional ideas for getting the most out of your teams. Maybe you are looking to break through to the playoffs for the first time or desiring a systematic approach for motivating your players.

Whatever your motivation as a coach, I challenge you to put GET MOR^{3}EE into practice with your team during your next season. Each season your team is a new mystery, and the GET MOR^{3}EE formula can help you decipher the clues to solve the mystery and find the keys for unlocking your team's greatest potential.

Let's look briefly at each property of the GET MOR^{3}EE formula.

MOTIVATION: Motivation is the ability to inspire someone to something more. To truly inspire is to breathe life into another. Another factor is getting to know your people and understanding their motives. Discovering their "have-to" and "want-to."

OWNERSHIP: Ownership is the value individuals bring to a role and the equity they create in it. When individuals avoid taking ownership, they are just consuming and using everything and everyone around them and not adding value to themselves or anyone else. They are not building equity in themselves or within the team. Equity is where there is worth. Equity is valuable. We need to instill a sense of ownership in our people, and they will increase their investment into the team. The concept of ownership is the foundation of R^3.

R^3 = RESPONSIBILITY, RESPECT, REWARDS: This is illustrated as R to the third power in the GET MOR^{3}EE acronym to help the leader understand that these three things aren't to be added upon each other sequentially but are to be thought of as multiplied together to a power. Power is the appropriate word, because responsibility, respect, and rewards are all powerful drivers in a high achiever. Together they are explosive. As a leader, I need to understand how to align these needs of the individual with the mission of the organization. The better I can do this, the higher potential payout from the individual.

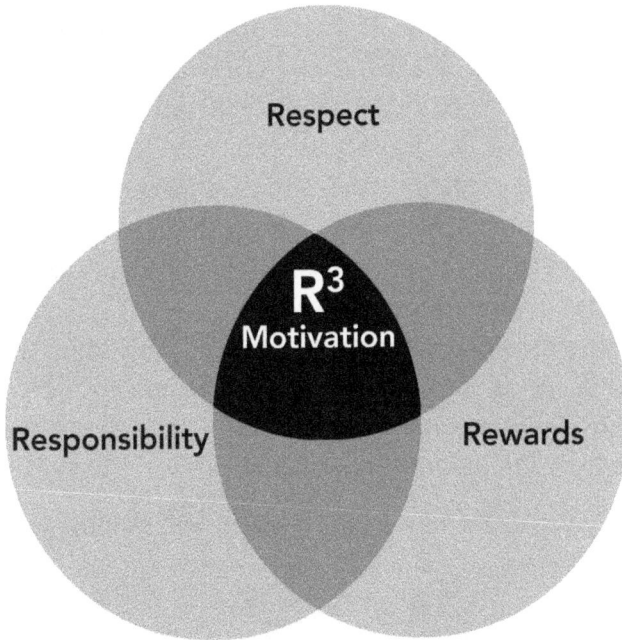

Diagram 1: The Three Rs and Motivation

RESPONSIBILITY: The individual made an investment and accepted some ownership; now give them some responsibility. Set a standard and present a clear picture of the role. Explain the duties of the role. Convey your expectations of them in that role and ask them if they are ready to accept ownership of those responsibilities. Confirm their commitment.

RESPECT: Respect is a vital part of any relationship and this process. It's no coincidence that respect is at the heart of this formula. Respect fosters the goodwill of the organization. Without respect the formula is unsustainable. It would be akin to ripping the battery out of your car. It disrupts the function of all the other components and takes the energy. If you have a person who will not respect the process, the people, or the standard, he or she will hold you back from reaching your team's full potential. I can always work with respect.

REWARDS: What is the payoff for their efforts? What is the ROI (return on investment)? What's the incentive? What's the benefit? A reward can be tangible or intangible. Have you as the leader aligned the reward with the work? Have you portrayed the reward as valuable and worth their efforts and commitment?

ENCOURAGEMENT: Belief from a leader is a huge component of the encouragement piece of GET MOR³EE. Encouragement is powerful and necessary for an organization to flourish and grow. Accountability is also encouragement. As leaders we need to recognize the power of consistent encouragement and the power of encouragement through accountability. Encouragement is the fuel that leads to empowerment.

EMPOWERMENT: Empowerment is an individual's self-confidence to take initiative in doing more, which fuels creativity, imagination, and passion and creates even greater momentum and motivation.

MOMENTUM: If you combine all the elements as you cycle through the GET MOR³EE formula, then you will begin to build momentum with individual players and ultimately with your team.

THE GET MOR³EE CYCLE OF SUSTAINABLE GROWTH AND EMPOWERMENT

Motivation

Performance

Empowerment

Growth

Ownership

Time

Momentum

COACHING IS THE EXPONENTIAL MULTIPLIER OF TALENT AND POTENTIAL.

Encouragement

R³ Responsibility Respect Rewards

Diagram 2: The GET MOR³EE Formula Cycle

GET MOR³EE is a formula for creating sustainable growth in the people you are leading. As you cycle through all the elements in the GET MOR³EE formula you begin to build momentum. Imagine that each time you reach empowerment, motivation leaps forward, and the cycle turns a little bit faster. As you coach your players through each turn, the ability, attitude, and confidence of the individual grows. The growth may seem small at first—almost invisible in the beginning. But as a coach, you continue encouraging the growth of your players' talents and budding potential. Eventually, almost out of nowhere, breakthrough occurs. The consistent application and alignment of these elements in the personal development of your players result in the exponential growth of their talents and potential. You will see a higher rate of growth than what naturally would have occurred. When a team of players are all experiencing breakthrough, then you have built massive momentum. Positive momentum is a coach's best friend.

WHAT ARE THE QUALITIES OF A GET MOR³EE COACH?

A GET MOR³EE coach:

- is highly people-oriented and highly results-oriented.[7]
- is a give-more coach. A GET MOR³EE coach loves to win.
- is a championship coach. A GET MOR³EE coach is a coach who cares.
- seeks knowledge. A GET MOR³EE coach pursues excellence.
- is an enlarger. A GET MOR³EE coach is a maximizer.
- is inspirational. A GET MOR³EE coach is an instiller.
- is a leader. A GET MOR³EE coach is a planner.
- is visionary. A GET MOR³EE coach is a problem solver.
- sees things as they are, while maintaining unwavering faith that they will succeed.

The next chapters discuss each property of the GET MOR³EE formula, detailing the principles, providing examples, and sharing stories to help you make the connection to why each of these properties is vital to applying the formula effectively. "**Motivation**" and "**Encouragement**" are the longest chapters because your vision for your team and how you fuel your team are extremely important. The **ownership** chapter sets up the R³ motivational properties. I divide **responsibility, respect,** and **rewards** into three separate chapters to focus in on each property with you and give

---

7. Michael Zigarelli, *Ordinary People, Extraordinary Leaders* (Gainesville: Synergy Publishers, 2002), states that an extraordinary leader is highly people-oriented and highly results-oriented.

them their due, but these should really be thought of as R^3 and multiplied together. **Empowerment** of our people is the product we are seeking with the GET MOR^{3}EE formula.

CHAPTER THREE
MOTIVATION

You have to recognize where you are but not lose the vision of where you want to go.

We start with motivation.

When you think of the role of a coach, what is one of the first things that should be in any coach's job description? What is one of the top qualities? The ability to motivate. "Influence" is another term we often hear. I've heard leadership guru John Maxwell make this statement: "Leadership is influence, nothing more, nothing less."[8] Influence is the capacity to have an effect on the character, development, or behavior of someone or something. To **affect** the character ... the development ... the behavior.

So, it seems that a coach's capacity to motivate someone is of utmost importance to his or her effectiveness as a leader and a coach. Earlier, I shared the Alpine Institute study that found that only 36 percent of coaches have effective motivational technique training. If you are going to be truly effective at any level of coaching, then increasing your capacity to positively motivate people is an imperative skill for succeeding with your players and teams. If we understand that one of our primary roles is that of a motivator, then to be effective as a coach, leader, and motivator we need to get to know people and understand what motivates them.

We seek to inspire people through motivation, which I liken to breathing life into another. To motivate is to provide someone with a motive for doing something or to stimulate a person's interest or enthusiasm for doing something.

---

8. John Maxwell said this during conferences at my church, Christ Fellowship, in Palm Beach Gardens, Florida.

"The secret of weariness and nervous disease in the natural world is a lack of a dominating interest." (Oswald Chambers)[9]

The primary role of any coach is to grab the players' interest and motivate them. I think the preceding quote illustrates this principle perfectly. Can you create an environment that can dominate a player's interest? The coach has one of the best platforms to seize a player's undivided attention. When your players are with you at training or games, they enter a world free of the distractions of cell phones, television, and other devices. There may not be another human being in this person's life who commands as much quality, focused, undistracted, and undivided time as the coach.

But isn't it the coach's primary role, you say, to teach the game? To show the player how to properly shoot a free throw or the proper technique for holding a tennis racquet? Isn't it his or her ability to draw up Xs and Os and create suffocating defensive schemes? To teach tactics and formations?

Renowned sports psychologist Bob Rotella shared this thought in the book *Golf Is Not a Game of Perfect*: "The more I coached, the more convinced I became that the Xs and Os that obsessed many coaches were rather less important than the attitudes and confidence they instilled in their players."[10]

I've observed many great coaches with limited understanding of the game they were coaching turn their teams into winners and get more out of their teams than the person who played for 15 years, because they understood how to motivate their players. The players already knew how to play the game or would discover how to do it better than the coach could teach them, but the coach provided the environment for the players to play, compete, and discover their ability to win. The coach saw the embers glowing, gave them some oxygen, and then stoked the flame—and then the players threw gasoline on it. So we start with motivation.

I share this quote of mine with you in a few different chapters throughout the book because I believe it speaks so loudly. It also is relevant to every property of the GET MOR³EE formula:

9. Oswald Chambers, *Not Knowing Whither* (London: Simpkin Marshall, 1934).
10. Bob Rotella, *Golf Is Not a Game of Perfect* (New York: Simon and Schuster, 1995).

Power comes from the vision, not the volume. How much you say and how loud you say it will never be as inspiring as what you say. How much you say and how loud you say it will never be as inspiring as the vision you cast.

A compelling vision calls out much louder than you can ever speak. When you are able to communicate a clear and compelling vision, people rise up on their own to follow it. They are self-motivated by the mission to invest their time, expertise, and energy towards the cause. The motivation is no longer about you and the length of your conversation or volume of your speech but about the vision you have for them. You can make mistakes and be wrong on occasion, as we eventually will be, and it won't matter, because your players are focused no longer on you but on the vision you have for their lives. They become committed to it, and thus to you and the team. They give more and risk more than you can ever ask of them because they are empowered by the rewards of the vision. They let you lead them. They follow you because you gave them the power to see and believe in the vision you set before them.

I've known a good friend of mine for almost a quarter century, since our days at Palm Beach Atlantic University. Our wives use to work together, we were business partners at one time, and now we both coach for The King's Academy High School in West Palm Beach, Florida. Jake Webb is the head varsity boys' lacrosse coach at The Kings Academy, and I coach varsity boys' soccer. Jake didn't play a lick of lacrosse as a kid, but Jake is a competitor. We used to play intramural sports against each other in college, so I know. Many times in coaching I'll lose a battle to win the war. Jake is going to try to win all the battles and the war.

He probably never played soccer as a kid. I've been playing all my life. The first year my son was playing pee-wee soccer, we were in the playoff finals of five- and six-year-old coed soccer. I'll never forget it, because it was so fascinating. Our teams were in the finals, and I had a good team. They had been fantastic all season. I think the only time we lost was when we were missing players and playing down a man. We were in this championship finals game against Jake's team. Now again, we are talking about mostly five- and six-year-olds, so this was like super fun, and we were just having a great time of it as players, coaches, and parents. There were some rules on substitutions, I think, at the time, or maybe we had our own internal rules—can't recall exactly—but what I remember is his strategy. Every time I subbed a couple of my better players out, he would immediately sub all his best players back in. I mean, I noticed this within the first couple of times it happened. He had scouted us and worked out a strategy, a winning strategy, in five- to six-year-olds recreational soccer to win the championship in a sport he never played. It still makes me laugh.

Fast-forward ten years, and Jake becomes the lacrosse coach at The King's Academy, probably a year or two before I'm hired, having never picked up a stick, or whatever they call it, until maybe his kids got interested and started playing. Jake is coaching against former Division I and professional lacrosse players now turned coaches at schools with very deep lacrosse programs and a lot of financial support. In 2018, he takes a team of freshmen and a couple of soccer kids from our team who had never played lacrosse and goes almost undefeated. I think it was 17 wins and 2 losses in his third season coaching lacrosse. The team he lost to twice was the number one ranked team in the state by Maxpreps at the time and finished the past two seasons as the number four ranked team in the state. Again, he has never played this game. This past season he goes across the state and defeats the IMG boys' lacrosse team. IMG kids are paying thousands of dollars—sorry, tens of thousands of dollars—a year to be trained by the best lacrosse coaches in the country with the idea that they can get into the top D1 colleges and play professionally, and they probably will. Jake's kids win!

What I observed in Jake years ago is that he understands how to motivate kids and he's passionate about doing it. He makes sure that they take ownership and responsibility for their actions on and off the field; models respect; and keeps his eye on the prize. He's a massive encourager, keeping players accountable, and empowers the kids to get more! He's obviously learned more about the game and prepared himself further through study and the people he brings in around him, but he has to empower and inspire those people to be creative and imaginative and achieve more because they play the game better than he ever has. He wins more because he gets more out of his talent than the coaches with more talent. I'll say it again. He wins more because he gets more out of his talent—his players—than the coaches with more talented players. IMG should technically have a team with more talented players, more resources, and more time to develop their athletes. Give Jake a competitive synchronized swimming or water polo team or ultimate Frisbee team, and I think he would create winners in those sports too because he builds the people within whatever the program is.

COACH ROB MENDEZ, ESPN HERO

I recently read the "Dear Football" letter written by Coach Rob Mendez in the *ESPN The Magazine* Heroes edition.[11] It is a worthwhile read for everyone, but especially for coaches. Coach Mendez is the 2019 recipient of the Jimmy V Award for Perseverance. Born without arms and legs, Rob Mendez has always been fascinated by football and in his first head coaching position led the junior varsity (JV) football squad at Prospect High School in Saratoga, CA, to an 8–2 record.

Coach Mendez's letter is inspiring, and the first thing that jumped out at me was that in his freshman year of high school, a coach invited him to be a part of the team. We can't look back and see whether or not we would be reading this letter from Rob Mendez without that coach's invitation. I'm sure he would have found his way here. It's obvious though that the coach's invitation was a monumental moment in his life and that he was thankful for it.

I think the athletes we coach are always looking for an invitation. Not just to be a part of the team, but an invitation from their coach to pursue dreams and excellence. An invitation to invest everything and fail miserably, laugh it off, learn, and go again. It's just sport, right? Right? They are looking for an invitation to be a champion on and off the field and to know that someone believes in them.

Coach Mendez found that his belief in his players translated to his players' belief in him, even though he had physically never played a down of football in his life. He can explain Xs and Os from running thousands of plays in his mind. His ability to inspire and motivate his players will always be far more important than his ability to demonstrate technique.

Some might say Coach Mendez is at a disadvantage, having never physically played the game. What he lacks in game experience and physical ability might actually be what makes him an effective coach. He

11. Rob Mendez, "It's Only the Beginning," ed. Wayne Drehs, *ESPN The Magazine* (June 18, 2019), https://www.espn.com/espys/story/_/id/26974520/espys-2019-high-school-football-coach-rob-mendez-receive-jimmy-v-award-perseverance.

found purpose in coaching these kids. He will never be able to rely on his technical prowess or playing résumé. Rob Mendez's coaching strengths will always be inspiration and belief, which may be the greatest gifts a coach can bestow upon players.

There are several different characteristics that come to mind when I say the word "motivate." As a starting point, I think as a leader it's always easier to motivate a person when you understand **their** motivations. What motivates them as a person? What is motivating them to be a part of your team?

There is a motivation that brings a person into an initial introduction with you. Looking at it through an athletics lens, there is a motivation that brings a student-athlete into an initial introduction with you. There is some motivation on the part of student athletes to try to make your team. Do they love the sport? Love to compete? Have a friend on the team? Need a school PE credit? Is a parent pushing them into it? (And I don't mean to make that sound like a negative thing. Many great success stories start with "Well, my dad took me, and I didn't want to go but then fell in love with it.") Someone took them by the hand and gave them a little motivation and a little encouragement, they took a liking to it, and then they began to pick up a glove or golf club or book on their own, and they became empowered and gained some self-motivation to continue.

Let's think about it from a business perspective for a moment. Say you as an employer are interviewing prospective hires. Do the prospective hires seem to have an interest in the product or service you provide? Do they enjoy the industry? Do they just love your company and want to be a part of it? Do they have a friend or someone who works there and is encouraging them to come work with you? Do they excel at certain tasks and enjoy doing them? Do they just need a job? Do they have bills and need to make a certain amount of money?

The point I'm making is that as a leader or coach you need to get to know the people in your care. And I use the word "**care**" intentionally because consciously or subconsciously many people are trusting you as the figurehead—your company, your school, your athletic department, the parents of the players, and the athletes you've made a part of your team.

I say "figurehead" because sometimes you are installed there and you haven't really decided whether you are going to own that position and lead yet. The good news is you can make the decision to coach right now. It is not too late to start investing into the people in your care and being interested in how they do their job, their productivity, and how they are performing individually and within the team—and to help them do better, be better, and to get more out of themselves.

HAVE TO AND WANT TO

Let's jump back to the descriptions I gave of what motivates a person. If you'll notice, there are two distinct differences in those descriptions. The individual loves the sport and loves to compete. The individual **wants** to be there, **wants** to win and play. The individual needs a PE credit, or someone is making them try out. They **have** to be there to get that PE credit so they can graduate or **have** to at least try out or Mom and Dad won't give them the GI Joe with the kung-fu grip.

There are have-tos **and** or want-tos, and as the coach, leader, and influencer it's your job to learn and understand what have-tos and or want-tos are motivating the people around you.

I remember when one of my colleagues interviewed a real estate agent and asked him how and why he had built his business up and, if he looked way back, what had motivated him to do it in the first place. I expect that my colleague was anticipating a deep business breakdown of how and why, and I was probably expecting something else as well, but this real estate agent just simply replied, "I had to. I didn't have a choice. I had six kids at home I had to provide for." My colleague was taken aback and stumbled and tried to probe a little deeper with another couple of questions, but again the real estate agent just replied, "I didn't have a choice." He had a powerful **have-to**.

I'm not saying one is better than the other, and having a little bit of both may be best, but I do think at times one may need to be amplified more than the other to create a more powerful self-motivation and drive.

Either one can be powerful in its own way. At different times and different stages of life one can become more powerful than another. As leaders, one of our roles is helping people discover which one it is and reminding them of it periodically, and that may be all the motivation that an individual needs.

"The only thing worse than running is not having something to run for." This is a quote attributed to five-time NCAA Division III National

Championship head women's soccer coach at Messiah College, Scott Frey, after one of his players said she would never look back and miss the summer workouts.[12]

I've heard similar interviews with top athletes like Tom Brady, Cristiano Ronaldo, Michael Phelps, and Bernhard Langer. Even after they've "made it," won a few Super Bowls, scored 600 goals and been signed for record transfer deals, won a dozen Olympic gold medals, or won countless Senior Tour championships in a row, when asked why they keep going and keep pressing, the response is "I **have to** improve. I **want to** be the best. I **want to** win. I **want to** beat you." They have a powerful **have-to** or **want-to**. Even in what is supposed to be the declining years of their careers they have seemingly improved their performance. How? Why? They continue to create and find have-tos and want-tos to run for.

THE BLIND SIDE

There is a scene in the movie *The Blind Side* where the characters are at what is portrayed to be one of the first football practices for Michael Oher.[13] If you recall the movie, they have been trying to get him to play football because he is just a huge dude. So, in this scene he is playing offensive left tackle in practice, and he's just getting beat. He's the biggest guy out there but just looks soft. The head coach yells out to him, "Oher! You got a hundred pounds on Collis, and you can't keep him out of our backfield?!" The camera pans over to S.J., the little brother in the movie, sitting on the bleachers filming as Sandra Bullock's character walks up to the top of the bleachers to sit with her son and asks, "What's with the camera?" S.J. replies, "Michael does better when he can see what he's supposed to be doing." They run another play, and Michael horse-collars a defender as he goes by and throws him to the ground. The coach, a little frustrated, blows the whistle and, as he comes down from the platform he's observing from, calls Michael out. "Oher, come here, son." The coach meets Michael and grabs him by his shoulder pads. He gets real close to show him the technique needed to block and not get a penalty called on him and, as the coach explains, to keep Coach from getting mad at an unnecessary penalty. He finishes and sends him back to the huddle.

---

12. Michael Zigarelli, *The Messiah Method* (Maitland: Xulon Press, 2011).
13. *The Blind Side*, directed by John Lee Hancock, written by John Lee Hancock and Michael Lewis (Warner Brothers, 2009).

At this point, Sandra Bullock's character, Leigh Anne Tuohy, starts making her way out of the bleachers towards the practice field in her high heels and asks her son, S.J., to watch her stuff. As she is making her way, the coach stands with an assistant waiting for them to run the next play and says, "Well, at least he will look good coming off the bus. They'll be terrified until they realize he's a marshmallow. Looks like Tarzan, plays like Jane."

Right about this time Leigh Anne comes walking by the head coach and pats the coach on his rear and says, "Gimme a minute, Bert," as she is about to interrupt practice. The coach is like, "We're in the middle of practice, Leigh Anne!" And she replies, "Thank me later." She walks over to Michael, grabs him by a little sliver of his jersey, and pulls him over to the side. The exchange goes like this: "Michael, do you remember when we went to that horrible part of town to buy you those dreadful clothes? And I was a little bit scared and you told me not to worry about it because you had my back? If anyone tried to get to me you would have stopped them, right?" Michael replies, "Yes, ma'am." She continues, "And when you and S.J. were in that car wreck, what did you do to the airbag?" "Stopped it," Michael replies. "You stopped it," she reinforces. "This team is your family, Michael, and you have to protect them from those guys." She points at the defense. Leigh Anne then pulls the quarterback and running back over and gives Michael the image that the players are his family like she and S.J. are and asks him to protect them like he would their family. She finishes with "Are you going to protect the family, Michael?" and he responds with a smile through his helmet, "Yes, ma'am."

Now although this scene didn't happen in the real-life story of Michael Oher, I love it because it paints a great picture of the motivational piece of knowing what's at the core of someone and what motivates them. Sandra Bullock's character basically reached right into Michael's core in this scene and touched something that motivated him and then related it to the people around him and his job as a left tackle. To protect his teammates as his loved ones and family is displayed as one of his core natural instincts. The movie portrays that scene as kinda flipping the switch for him; Michael Oher turns into a bad man and starts flattening the defensive line, and he goes on to have a very successful college and NFL career.

The point is that Leigh Anne got to know Michael—she observed him and understood a little of what motivated him and some of his core fears and what he cared about. Coach is screaming and yelling, and Michael can't hear him, but Leigh Anne connects what his role is in the team and game to what motivates Michael and gives him a visual of how to apply it to the role he's in and help the team.

THE SAFE STOOL

This season at a coaches' dinner Jake Webb shared a story of something he has been doing with his high school lacrosse team called the "safe stool." Players take turns before a game or practice to sit on the stool and share whatever they want. It's meant to be a place safe from ridicule or judgment. Jake shared that it's been a powerful thing in the locker room as kids have been opening up and have even broken down crying on the stool while sharing some of the burdens or even tragedies in their lives. Jake explained that he had no clue some of these things were going on in his players' lives. Do you think that knowing about some of these life situations can help Jake relate to and motivate his players more effectively?

SELF-MOTIVATION

I generally try to look for self-motivated people. People who already have some motivation, some have-to or want-to that is driving them. You don't have to be on them constantly to do the general tasks. Regularly getting to practice on time isn't an issue for them. They stay in shape and practice in the offseason on their own with no prompting. They gladly help others around them.

Now here is the key point for you as the coach: **All** people are motivated by something. That's why it's even more important that as a leader you understand what that something is. Because if it doesn't align with where you're going, then the next question is, Can you align the individual's motivation to your organizational goals so that both the individual and the organization are served?

If not, or if you can't discover a motivation that can align the two, even if this person is a super-talented contributor it may be best for you as the leader to encourage him or her to pursue something else. Maybe you even need this person in your organization, but while listening to the person's motivations you discover that he or she may be better served elsewhere. As a leader, you may be negligent in the care of your players if you don't encourage them to look at other options that may better serve them in their long-term goals. If they decide to stay with you, then that's their decision, and then you run with them because they've then made the commitment to forgo all other options and stick with you.

What about the less talented individuals who seem to lack self-motivation? Do you just cast them aside? Maybe they just haven't connected to their have-to or want-to. Can you help them discover one? Can you help them find a place in the team where they can make a unique contribution?

There are very few "10s" in any area of life. There was only one Pelé. There is only one Messi. There is only one Cristiano Ronaldo. These players are the elite. Mia Hamm is the name from my generation in women's soccer that jumps out at me. We recognize them in other sports. Michael Jordan and LeBron James in basketball. Michael Phelps in swimming. Tiger Woods, Jack Nicklaus, and Annika Sorenstam in golf. Jackie Joyner-Kersee in track and field. Babe Ruth, Derek Jeter, Mike Trout, and Bryce Harper in baseball. They call Tom Brady "the G.O.A.T." (the greatest of all time). Some would call these players "special." Even at the highest levels of business, academia, and athletics there are only a few of the elite. They can seemingly **will** your team to win at times. Having one of these players can lead a team to the top echelon of your sport. There are very few of these players in the world, and you may never coach one.

Then there is the next tier of very good players, who have either strong talent or a strong work ethic or some combination of both that has brought them to this level. They produce consistently good performances and sometimes great performances. They can take you a long way and transform a team. Having a few of these players can make life easy for a manager or coach.

Then there are the contributors—the role players. And you need the contributors. Your team needs the contributors. Remember I said that there are very few elite players in the world and you may never have one on your team? You'll probably have many more very good players. With some dedication by the player, committed coaching, the proper environment, and the right opportunities, these players can have elite level performances at times. But in all cases, the elite and the very good need the help and the contributions of the role players to win and be successful.

Michael Phelps is the most decorated Olympic athlete of all time. In order to be honored with that moniker he needed the help of his US swim teammates in relays to win 12 of his 28 medals. He holds the all-time record with 23 Olympic gold medals, and 10 of those were won with teammates in the relay events. All of the elite golfers mentioned had coaches. And every one of them had a caddie on their bag for every single one of their professional victories. To win those NBA Championship Finals trophies, Michael Jordan had Scottie Pippen. LeBron James had Dwayne Wade and Chris Bosh. In all the championship stories on ESPN, you always hear the story of the contributions of the role players in their victory seasons.

Tom Brady is the winningest championship quarterback of all time, winning six NFL Super Bowls. Throughout his NFL career, though, he is also considered to have had maybe the greatest football coach of all time coaching him in Bill Belichick. Bill Belichick has eight Super Bowl rings as a coach in the NFL. Many people say the most impressive part of his job with the Patriots is bringing a new group of players together year after year and motivating everyone, from the stars to the one-season role players, to align on a singular mission and getting the best out of every player, whether on the field for one play or sixty plays.

So, this is the question for you, Coach: Can you tap into the less talented role players and turn them into productive contributors? Do you have a formula or methodology to help you be consistent in tapping into your players' full potential, or are you just winging it?

CREATING FIRSTS

I'll share a story from my first season as the boys' head varsity coach at The Kings Academy, a small Christian high school in West Palm Beach, Florida. In one of our first games of the year we were playing American Heritage of Delray. Talented players. Many of them were playing for what US Soccer calls the development academy (D.A.). To make the D.A. in an area you pretty much need to be the best of the best, and they had many of those elite players and top players from other top club programs. I didn't know this at the time, but in our school history our boys' soccer team had never defeated American Heritage. They had entered our district I think a few years prior, and if you looked back at their history, they had several state championships and state runner-up appearances and a track record of being really good. Not just good, but great.

On my team that year I had only one true forward. A forward is generally your goal scorer in soccer, your frontline attacking position. I could shape out the rest of the team, but I had no other forwards. So I took three or four kids who had never played forward. Most of them were defenders, and I think two of them had barely played organized soccer in their life. I told them I was going to train them to be my forwards. They looked at me a little baffled, as did the other players on the team, and I just said, "Let's work at it. I don't expect you to play sixty minutes a game or even score goals, but I know you can give me five, ten, or twenty productive minutes a game that can help the team." They had some athletic ability, and best of all they were willing to do whatever I asked of them, even if they didn't quite understand.

I explained to them what I needed them to do. Being the top line attackers, there was no expectation on them to score goals, which is different than what you might tell most strikers, but I knew that wasn't their strength. Asking them to do it might have been too much pressure and hurt their performance. Their job was to run. Run and pressure the other team's defenders relentlessly. Since I was playing with only two forwards and I had four or five of these guys, I told them, "Just give me your all and run and pressure until you can't run 100 percent anymore, and I'll sub in the next guy." And they did. In that first game against American Heritage, a converted defender, a midfielder, and two guys who had barely played soccer were my forwards. Every 10 minutes or so I'd sub them, and they'd run. In doing so they never allowed the other team to have a good staging area to build an attack. Our opponents were positioned into hitting balls at us from 40 yards out, which played to our strengths because we had a goalkeeper who went on to be a United Soccer Coaches All-American that season. We scored on a corner kick midway through the second half and held on for the win.

Afterwards, the coach Jonathan Frias, whom I've come to know and respect and who was also coaching his first season with American Heritage, came over to congratulate me and say that his boys were shocked by our performance. They said we looked different. It was pretty much the same team, but we were now getting more out of every single player, and it took that to win.

American Heritage went on to beat us in the district final, and the next season they went on to win the state championship with that same team. Our ability to have a victory against such a strong team was predicated on the ability of our role players to contribute in ways they didn't even know they could. We established that we were willing to give players the opportunity to contribute even in the big games and were willing to invest in them to get more. This was the start of our journey of eventually winning the district championship in our third try against American Heritage.

We live in a world that is now constantly competing for the attention of our youth. Coaches are going through the motions and have become unengaged and lack passion. Are you willing to be inspirational? Your players need visionary leadership and a compelling mission. Can you give that to them, Coach? Are you willing to?

GET MOR³EE: REMEMBER YOUR MOTIVES. OWN THE STRUGGLES. KEEP YOUR EYE ON THE PRIZE. ALLOW ACCOUNTABILITY TO FUEL YOU, NOT LIMIT YOU. LET IT ALL EMPOWER YOU.

SCOUTING REPORT LESSONS

▶ **You have to recognize where you are but not lose the vision of where you want to go.**

▶ To inspire means to breathe life into another person.

▶ Get to know your players. Develop the relationship.

▶ Understand how powerful have-tos and want-tos can motivate an individual. Help your players discover their have-to and want-to motivations.

▶ Help them see how their have-tos and want-tos can align with the organizational goals.

▶ Motivating the elite and very good players can be easy. How do you include and motivate your role players?

COACHES' BOX: GET MORE WITH A QUESTIONNAIRE

I give my players a questionnaire at the beginning of each season. I have them fill out their contact information, and then I ask questions about their favorite soccer player and team. Have they played soccer anywhere else, and do they still play now? How long have they been playing? Do they play any other sports? Where were they born? This helps me know if they are local or possibly even an international student or moved from another country. Why do they want to play for our team? What are their goals for themselves and the team? This gives me a basis of information on which to strike up a conversation or to relate a lesson that I'm trying to convey to something that is relevant to them. It helps me know their possible depth of understanding. If they are from a different country, then I may need to keep cultural differences in mind when interacting with them.

For example, the German exchange students we've had were in such a deep-rooted soccer culture in Germany that it can be very different for them when they come to play in the United States. I notice that each time there is a period of adjustment to the style, language, and the intensity of our season. It can take a while for them to buy in to what we are doing, and it can be frustrating for the other players who have been in the program. It's a delicate balance between understanding that time is needed to adapt and getting everyone on the same page as soon as you can.

One of my German exchange students sent me this text after our season this past year: *"Coach, I just want to say thank you for this great season and that you gave me so much playing time. I saw how much time you spend for this team to set everything up like practice and especially film. I had many coaches already, but I never had a coach who is so passionate about his job, and I really appreciate that. It was a great season, and I hope I see you next year when I come back for a practice at homecoming."*

CHAPTER FOUR
OWNERSHIP

When we think of ownership, we tend to visualize ownership of material things. I own this house. I own this car. That's my pen. I have title to it, and it has some value to me. You can own a business. A sport's team. A patent. Art. You traded time for money or money for time to earn this item, so it has value to you. You care about the object and how it's maintained or represented to others. There is worth. The greater the value we perceive it to have, the greater thought, care, and concern we generally give to it. So why say "ownership"? What does that have to do with the philosophy of the GET MOR³EE formula?

Well, in general, throughout society, people take better care of things that they own—things that they have a physical title to. They put in more effort. They invest more time and money if they have ownership and ownership of all or some of the return on investment. They put in more mind power. They think about it more, and they tend to look to add value to others in the community around them and the object they own. They hope that in doing so others will become just as or more invested, and the value of what they own will increase, or there will be other returns or benefits resulting from their ownership and investment.

This parable shared in the Gospel of John in the Bible conveys exactly how an invested person versus an uninvested person will treat your team:

> "I am the good shepherd. The good shepherd lays down his life for the sheep. The hired hand is not the shepherd and does not own the sheep. So when he sees the wolf coming, he abandons the sheep and runs away. Then the wolf attacks the flock and scatters it. The man runs away because he is a hired hand and cares nothing for the sheep." (John 10:11–13 NIV)

The wolf can be interpreted as the hard times and struggles that will eventually visit your team. The good shepherd in my comparison is like the invested player or coach who is committed and stands with the team when times are hard and it is under attack. Such coaches and players cast aside their own ambitions and desires for the love of the team. They have a strong sense of ownership in the team. The hired hand is like uninvested players or coaches who abandon the team when conflict or adversity arrives because they've taken no ownership in the team. Their love of self is greater than their desire for the team. The uninvested player or coach has developed low to no ownership in the team.

BECOMING AN OWNER

I heard Tony Robbins say in an interview that "the number one financial decision a person can make is to become an owner instead of constantly using products or services."[14] For our purposes, if you are constantly a user, then you are a consumer and not an owner. By not being an owner, you are just consuming and using everything and everyone around you and not adding value to yourself or anyone else. You are not building equity in yourself or within the team. Equity is where there is worth. Equity is valuable.

How does this concept of ownership integrate into the GET MOR³EE formula? Today we hear people talk about "taking ownership." Corporate America and the government have grabbed on to this phrase to motivate employees or citizens to take on or feel a greater sense of responsibility for a task or project. In John F. Kennedy's inaugural presidential address in 1961, he appealed to the sense of ownership in the American people in this statement: "In your hands, my fellow citizens, more than in mine, will rest the final success or failure of our course."[15] A few paragraphs later, the 35th president of the United States of America delivered the famous line "And so, my fellow Americans: ask not what your country can do for you—ask what you can do for your country." This appeal to ownership from the leader of the United States to its citizens has been referred to again and again by leaders around the world when appealing to their constituents and is one of the most remembered famous speeches in modern history.

14. Gary Vee, "Tony Robbins, Unshakeable, Gratitude & Focusing on Your Steak," March 1, 2017, interview, https://www.youtube.com/watch?v=9O8haH2tHWY.
15. John F. Kennedy, "Inaugural Address," January 20, 1961.

Leaders are able to motivate individuals through visualizing their job or tasks or place in the team through the lens of ownership to place a greater value in the quality of their work and the resulting outcome. Some people feel a sense of ownership naturally. Others need help to grasp the concept of ownership of their work. If I can help my players visualize their work as the result of their efforts, then I can help them see how they own the recognition and returns from the outcome and the work involved. Because the players' names are on the roster, people know their affiliation with the team and program, and so what the players do, other people see—the names of the players are attached to their actions.

"A good name is to be chosen rather than great riches." (King Solomon, the wisest man who ever lived [Prov. 22:1 NKJV])

Within my sports team, I let the players know at the beginning and end of the season and remind them throughout the season that a championship at the end of the season is not owned by me. It is not my victory, and it's not because of me. I play a part, and I'm going to create an environment for them to have success, but where we are at the end of the season is strictly a result of the commitment and effort they put into improving as a player throughout the season. They can't rely on me to do it for them. It's the 22 players around you who determines how far you go, and you have to come every day with that understanding. The season has a finite end, and every minute and day that you waste, you can't get back.

Beginning with the end in mind, focus on getting the most out of every day and practice, and keep your eye on the prize, and the results will take care of themselves. If constantly striving to improve and get better, you have the power to make it a great season. Your name is on the roster, and everyone sees and knows that you're affiliated with the team or program. Own it. Make it yours.

EQUITY

Another way to convey ownership is by helping people understand what equity means and how it relates to them in respect to a role or position within an athletic team or even a for-profit organization. In financial terms, "equity" may be defined as how much value you have after subtracting liabilities. When people talk about putting sweat equity into something, they are talking about their efforts and time in creating value in a business or asset. Here is the part that we have to be able to convey as leaders to our people: in whatever role or position they step into in life, they are immediately building equity. And that equity can be positive or negative equity. I'll explain.

The moment you step into any role or position in life you immediately begin building equity with the people around you. You own the actions, effort, attitude, and the role, even if you haven't yet realized it. People around you automatically assign the responsibility and ownership of your role to you. You might as well take ownership and responsibility for building equity in that role because people assume you do. If you don't, you run the risk of creating negative equity with people, with the organization, and for yourself in life. After observing or interacting with you, people will assign a "value" to who you might be and how you performed.

I want to create positive equity. My grandfather and father said it this way: "Try to leave a place better than you found it." I think that applies to each of us with this concept of equity. Am I better, and did I grow my own personal equity in myself from where I started when I came into this role? I own my actions, effort, and attitude—so whatever role I'm in, I better take ownership and create value, or someone else will put a value on me. Everything I do reflects back on me.

DEFINING VALUE

Two things define value: who owns it, and how much someone is willing to pay for it. Many times, the value of the role in the organization is defined by the person in it, the person who owns it, and not the role itself.

During the recent 2019 FIFA Women's World Cup, Brazil was eliminated by France in a 2–1 overtime loss. After the game, an interview given by Marta, the Brazilian captain considered by many to be the greatest women's soccer player of all time, went viral on television and social media, with millions of views in just a few hours. To give you some background on Marta, she has been named FIFA World Player of the Year six times! She was the first woman to score in five different FIFA World Cups, and she holds the record for most goals scored at FIFA World Cup tournaments. For all of Marta's individual accomplishments through five World Cups, Marta and her Brazilian teammates have never finished better than second. They've never won a World Cup. Here is what Marta had to say when speaking out to young Brazilian girls in her native Portuguese after being eliminated by France in what most likely could be her last World Cup: "It's wanting more. It's training more. It's taking care of yourself more. It's being ready to play 90 plus 30 minutes ... Value it more. Cry in the beginning so you can smile in the end."[16]

"Value it more."

As a coach, how do I convey ownership and value to the players on my team? Here are a few tips.

- Paint the picture of ownership for the individual and team. Use visuals and stories.
- Give them room to own it. Allow them air to self-discover and make mistakes.
- Include them in the process. They'll value it more.
- Allow them to surprise you with the outcomes and results.

For leaders and coaches this can be hard to do because, hey, you've got some real ownership here as well. In the world of youth and high school coaching, if your ultimate focus is on helping the kids in your charge become better people and better equipped for life and to get more out of themselves, then it's easy to give up ownership of the result as well. As a coach, if you try to own the entire result, it's a lot of work for you, and the value of the victories isn't as high. You may get a trophy, but the value won't be as high because it won't be as rewarding for the players. When the players are highly invested, they take on more of the burden with the losses and receive a greater portion of the profit (confidence, recognition) with a win. With everyone more highly invested in the process, individuals take on a greater responsibility for their own improvement and development, which makes our roles and responsibilities as coaches easier. Players become more coachable and put in more effort, and we don't have to be barking at them all the time to get the results we want in practice. They'll go out and do it themselves.

---

16. "Brazil's Marta gives epic, inspirational message to the next generation: 'Cry in the beginning so you can smile in the end,'" *Fox Soccer*, June 23, 2019, https://www.foxsports.com/soccer/video/1555934787749.

"BUT COACH"

It's fairly easy to recognize the kids who haven't yet come to understand the ownership idea. They are generally the kids with the ready excuses. They think your name is "But Coach," and conversations tend to go something like this:

> You: "Hey, team, we will be meeting at 5 p.m. for our game tomorrow night."
>
> Non-ownership player: "But Coach, I don't think I can make it because my mom's second cousin's friend's sister's husband's aunt's dog had puppies and she needs to give them away because she found out her son doesn't like cats."
>
> You: "What? So why can't you make the game?"
>
> Non-ownership player: "Because my neighbors want to maybe get one of the puppies."
>
> You: "And...?"
>
> Non-ownership player: "Uh, ya, and I was going to maybe drive them to look at the puppies."
>
> You: "Can you go on Saturday when we don't have practice or a game?"
>
> Non-ownership player: "But Coach, all the cute puppies might be gone."
>
> You: "They are all cute! They're puppies!"

You get the idea.

This next one has been a staple conversation for me in every season. I'm using Key Club in the following example because it's the actual conversation I have annually. Just to be clear, I'm not knocking Key Club or any other club. I'm just sharing an example of another "But Coach" conversation.

> Me: "Practice starts at 3:30 p.m., team. We have some new tactics I want to review before the next game, so I need everyone here on time."
>
> Non-ownership player: "But Coach, I'll be late for practice because I have Key Club recycling tomorrow. It will only take like 30 minutes."

[Me thinking: *I can't believe I'm about to have this conversation again.*]

Me: "And why did you schedule that on a practice day?"

Non-ownership player: "Well, I thought you would rather me schedule it after school on a practice day and miss practice than on a game day, so I wouldn't be tired for the game."

Me: "Why would I ever want you to miss practice? If you're not at practice, then you won't know what to do when I call on you in a game. Schedule it on a day when we don't play until 7 p.m."

Non-ownership player: "But Coach, if I miss, they might kick me out of Key Club, and I need extracurriculars so I can get into college. If I don't, the colleges may not look at me."

Me: "Which do you think the college enrollment officer will consider more highly in your application, a list of the clubs you were in, or a recommendation letter from your coach commending you for being able to manage your academics, club, and community commitments while also maintaining high contribution and dedication to the team?"

I could go on, but you have your own version of those conversations. That's still one of my all-time favorites. I shouldn't be surprised, but I end up having that same conversation every season. If I could insert an emoji here it would be the one with the laughing tears face!

COACHES' BOX: LONG-TERM INVESTMENTS

For coaches truly invested in the development of players, the "But Coach" conversations can be frustrating because we know that if our players understood this ownership piece it would change their season and ultimately their future. Sadly, coming to understand ownership may not happen in a season or in multiple seasons for a player. We have to continue to be consistent, though, because we never know when the seeds we've planted will sprout. The ah-ha moment hits them, and then the potential we have to work with is now free, and then it gets real fun. That's the payoff. Even if the payoff doesn't come in our time with them, we just keep planting. Sometimes we're just the sower and someone else gets to enjoy the harvest.

I think many times as coaches we get caught up in the "credit" of results, so we invest in the short-term with players. We might sacrifice the relationship with a player or the benefit of learning for the quick fix of a possible win. We are maybe selfish with our time with the less talented players or the players that don't quite "get it" because we can't see the immediate payoff or benefit. I know it happens with me at times. I like to see even the smallest results or improvements in my players. It fires me up and gets me excited! It gives me a feeling of accomplishment! It is tangible feedback that what I am doing is working.

It can be difficult to have a long-term perspective when you might only coach a player for one or two years. The coach who is truly invested in the ultimate welfare of his or her players is able to balance both short-term effort and results with the long-term development of all the players on the team. Some of the best coaching is done off the field where no one will ever see it. There is no tangible way to account for it, but both the player and the coach intrinsically know it. I think coaches who understand and apply this type of balance with their players understand the following statement, which President Ronald Reagan kept on a small plaque on his desk in the Oval Office of the White House: "There is no limit to what a man can do or where he can go if he does not mind who gets the credit."[17]

Basketball coach John Wooden, who is considered the best college basketball coach of all time—and some would argue maybe the best coach ever—won 10 NCAA men's

---

17. "Reagan the Man," Ronald Reagan Presidential Foundation and Institute, accessed September 19, 2019, https://www.reaganfoundation.org/ronald-reagan/the-presidency/reagan-the-man/.

basketball championships, including an unprecedented streak of 7 in a row. At one point, the team won 88 men's basketball games in a row, which is a record most think will never be touched.

John Wooden took over the UCLA men's basketball program in 1948. It was 16 seasons of investing before Coach Wooden had his breakthrough moment and won his first NCAA national championship. Nine more would follow in the next 11 seasons.

The commitment to the consistent investment into the person is what leads to the eventual breakthrough, and some people take longer to develop than others, but when they do, the payoff can be exponential.

Warren Buffett, often considered the greatest investor of all time, made 99.7 percent of his fortune after the age of 52. He had spent over 30 years consistently investing before he had a massive breakthrough.[18]

OWN THE LOSSES

In the New Testament, "Coach Paul" teaches that

ADVERSITY DEVELOPS ENDURANCE, ENDURANCE DEVELOPS STRENGTH OF CHARACTER, CHARACTER STRENGTHENS OUR CONFIDENCE. (see Rom. 5:3–5)

I posted the following on LinkedIn in response to an article someone wrote about allowing kids to lose or fail, and I shared a picture of our team after they won the district championship.

So, these kids did this after STARTING this season 2–7–1. I'm thankful for the early struggles, as it showed us we were not yet good enough to accomplish the great goals we set. The adversity prepared us for the tougher challenges that lay ahead—when it really mattered. The boys OWNED the defeats and allowed

18. Grant Cardone, *The 10X Entreprenuer*, August 30, 2018, https://medium.com/the-10x-entrepreneur/warren-buffett-has-made-99-7-of-his-money-after-the-age-of-52-71e2ce04c347.

it to strengthen them. They FINISHED the season as district CHAMPIONS.

Own the failures. Own the losses. It's so easy to just try to dismiss the losses. We do that, right? We find an excuse for why we failed or lost. It was the economy, the markets, the field, the weather—but maybe, in that moment, we just weren't good enough. Maybe we didn't train hard enough or we were focused on the wrong things. Maybe we didn't prepare properly or have the right plan. Maybe we had a good plan and none of that other stuff matters and we just didn't execute. Whatever the reason for the loss, we have to look at ourselves in the mirror and own it.

Here's the most important lesson in this: If we are dismissive of the failures, dismissive of the losses, and we don't own them, then we lose and take another loss in the opportunity to learn from them. We miss the opportunity to learn from them and continue to make the same mistakes, leading to more losses, until we start owning them. Only then can we truly learn and change and hopefully do more, be more, have more, give more, live more, learn more, smile more, get more.

HOW OWNERSHIP TRANSFORMED A SEASON

The Kings Academy Varsity Boys' Soccer team I coach began the season with high expectations. We had a new system and looked amazing in practice. When we scrimmaged our JV team, we torched them. We looked unstoppable. Then we played our first preseason match.

Now we have always played in this one preseason tournament where we face teams that are a couple classes higher than us. Basically, the class system in high school assumes that if your school is larger and has more students, theoretically you have a larger player pool to pull from and thus maybe more talent opportunities. I have never won a preseason game, and I'm okay with it because I want us to be tested against schools with potentially more talent. That being said, our team stepped on the field for this preseason contest with a ton of confidence. I had veteran players anchoring our back line. I had multiple scoring threats—I felt like for the first time in three seasons—and a solid midfield system.

I think the final score was a 7–1 or so loss.

I believe it was Mike Tyson who famously stated, "Everybody has a plan until they get punched in the mouth." We got smoked. It completely exposed us. It destroyed all of our wonderful ideas. We tried not to lose heart and tested a few things in our next game, but the result was the same. A pretty solid loss. We found something we thought might work and jumped into it with a week of training before our first regular season game. The result was the same. We were four games into the season before we squeaked out a narrow 2–1 win to give us some hope going into the Thanksgiving break. It was another four games before our next win, and we gave up four goals in that game. Our defense was struggling, giving up over three goals a game on average. We were splitting time between two relatively inexperienced goalkeepers, trying to find the right fit. Our value was in scoring goals, which we were doing, but we were still losing.

I approached a couple of my captains and let them know we needed to make a switch. They accepted the calling, and they stepped into the defensive role full time, and the value of the position changed. They brought a different level of ownership to the position and went a step further to request the goalkeeper they wanted behind them the rest of the season. Together as a center-back partnership they added more value, to the point where we stopped giving up goals. We went from a goals against average of plus three to less than 0.5 heading into the playoffs. Up until this point we had zero shutouts during the season, but in the first game after the switch, we won and logged our first shutout. We would add five more shutouts, including three in our five playoff games. We shut out our opponents in the team's 1–0 win in the district championship game over the defending state champions and in a 1–0 victory in the regional quarterfinals to advance to the semifinals for only the second time in school history. Along the way, we faced the team that beat us 7–1 in that first preseason game. Missing three of our starters (including one of the captains who was now playing center back), we narrowly lost 2–1.

My center-back defenders had become infectious to a point where even when they weren't playing, their level of intensity and commitment was maintained. They were not impartial placeholders of that position but owned it. They made it their responsibility, beyond all else, to stop giving up goals. They took it upon themselves to have greater responsibility to encourage and cover the players around them, and the value of the position grew so much, to the point that we became a dominant team and won the district championship. Both of those center-back defenders, Cameron Stovel and Will Champlin, were named to the Palm Beach Post All-County First Team for boys' soccer. Two central defenders from the same team, essentially playing the same position, being recognized in the best eleven players in the county is not a regular occurrence. Will Champlin was later announced as the Palm Beach County Boys' Soccer Player of the Year and as a United Soccer Coaches All-State Team selection. The value of the position was greater because of who owned it.

GET MOR³EE: REMEMBER YOUR MOTIVES. OWN THE STRUGGLES. KEEP YOUR EYE ON THE PRIZE. ALLOW ACCOUNTABILITY TO FUEL YOU, NOT LIMIT YOU. LET IT ALL EMPOWER YOU.

SCOUTING REPORT LESSONS
- ▶ Invested players have a strong sense of ownership.
- ▶ Convey ownership of their role to all individuals on the team.
- ▶ Help them understand that they are building positive or negative equity every day.
- ▶ Help them understand that by taking ownership of their role and building equity they are adding to their value and the net worth of the team.
- ▶ Let them know it's okay to own the losses and failures. Otherwise they can't learn from them.

CHAPTER FIVE
R³: RESPONSIBILITY, RESPECT, AND REWARDS

As human beings, we instinctively seek some degree of responsibility, respect, and rewards. When I accept a job and take ownership of a role, I automatically know there are responsibilities that come with the role. I receive some responsibility I am seeking, and for taking on this responsibility and performing well I hope to receive some level of admiration and recognition—the old pat on the back or just a little respect. There are also some rewards I am seeking, which may be tangible or intangible, such as money or fame. Or maybe in my own internal rewards system I have a sense of accomplishment or acceptance, and that is my reward.

This R³ concept is illustrated as R to the third power in the GET MOR³EE acronym to help the leader understand that these three things aren't meant to be added upon each other sequentially but are to be thought of as multiplied together to a power. "Power" is the appropriate word, because responsibility, respects, and rewards are all individually powerful drivers in a high achiever. Multiplied together, they are a jet engine. As a leader, I need to understand how to align these three needs of the individual with the mission of the organization. A jet-propelled vehicle pointed in the wrong direction flies off course quickly. Motivation and ownership provide your team with direction and foundation. Align this foundational "MO" with R³ to create powerful motivation—"The Big MO" in your players.[19] The better I can do this, the higher the potential payout from the individual.

I expound upon the R³ (R to the third power) over the next three chapters, but motivation and ownership need to come first. To create

---

19. "The Big MO" refers to momentum. John C. Maxwell, in *The 21 Irrefutable Laws of Leadership* (Nashville: Thomas Nelson, 1998 and 2007), describes the Law of the Big MO and the benefits of momentum in leadership.

motivation, we "begin with the end in mind."[20] We create vision and direction. We establish where we want to go as a team and as individuals. This is when we discuss goals and mission. We could perform all the other functions in the GET MOR³EE formula very effectively but later find ourselves working really hard while moving in the wrong direction.

Understanding the concept of ownership is foundational to the effective motivational power of the R^3 properties. You can discuss and give responsibility to a person at any time, but it is important to have first instilled ownership—the sense of responsibility a player feels is then compounded by the sense of ownership in the results or process. Respect is a vital part of any relationship and this process, although the amount of respect an individual brings to the relationship or process is not nearly as powerful as when compounded by the idea of ownership. An individual's level of respect for themselves, the collective group, the process, the property, the equipment, and the building is much higher when viewed through the lens of ownership. You respect something much more when you see your name on it. Rewards are a powerful motivator, and many times the perceived rewards are enough to get a person to commit to becoming an owner in your team. Motivation and ownership set the stage for aligning the motivating factors of R^3 with your team. Aligning and multiplying these factors together lead to compounding motivational effects with the individuals you are leading and coaching.

Consider how two individuals invested in the same cause can power a team to a complete turnaround and a championship season. In this context, 1×1 does not equal 1 as it normally does in mathematics. When individuals take ownership of their role and invest deeply in their team, the math works something like this: $1 \times 1 = 3$. The same concept applies to R^3. In the GET MOR³EE formula, responsibility, respect, and rewards are separate properties, but they should be thought of as interconnected and working together, as in the example in diagram 1. Mathematically we think of it as R^3 (R to the third power), where instead of adding together responsibility, respect, and rewards, they are multiplied together, creating higher levels of motivation and exponential returns in the individual growth of talent and potential and team performance.

20. Stephen R. Covey, *The Seven Habits of Highly Effective People* (New York: Simon and Schuster, 1989). "Begin with the end in mind" is the second habit in the order of the seven habits.

Let's turn the page and go deeper with each of the three properties of R^3.

GET MOR³EE: REMEMBER YOUR MOTIVES. OWN THE STRUGGLES. KEEP YOUR EYE ON THE PRIZE. ALLOW ACCOUNTABILITY TO FUEL YOU, NOT LIMIT YOU. LET IT ALL EMPOWER YOU.

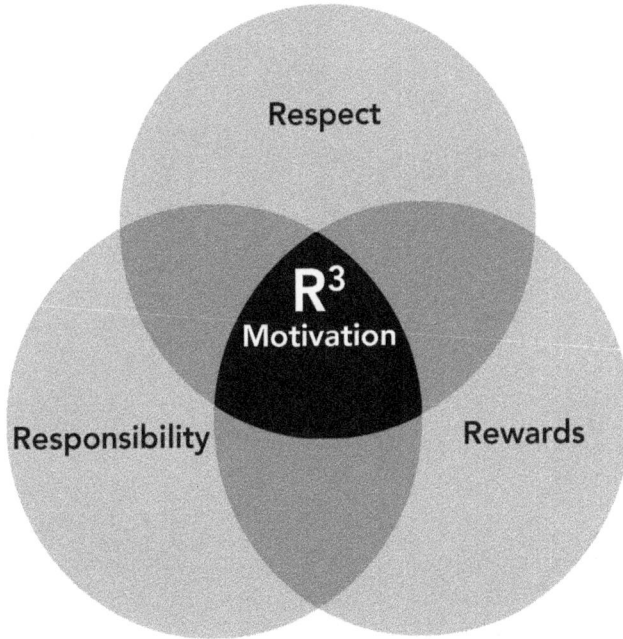

Diagram 1: The Three Rs and Motivation

CHAPTER SIX
RESPONSIBILITY

My number one responsibility is to motivate the players to succeed at whatever we define success to be.

Former dean of the Stanford Graduate School of Business Robert L. Joss states, "Too many leaders get caught up in thinking about power rather than responsibility to those they lead."[21] Coaches, managers, and leaders all have a responsibility to the people in their organization that is required as part of their job. A coach has a responsibility to his or her players to get more out of their talents and potential. Whatever you hope and desire to achieve as a coach is all rooted in this responsibility to GET MORE out of your players. This responsibility of the coach is at the core of the GET MOR^{3}EE formula.

I think we all are willing to take on a certain degree of responsibility. I would even say we want and need it. Now, I may be willing to take on more responsibility because I enjoy it and also because I may assume I'll receive a higher level of respect. It's also possible that I'll take on more responsibility because I hold a higher degree of respect for my organization, role, family, or boss. I may take on the additional responsibility because I have a higher sense of duty. The same applies for the perceived rewards I expect to receive. I choose to accept a role because of the rewards that are associated with the responsibility of the role.

One of the main functions of a coach is to delegate responsibility to others. In the book *Leading* by legendary Manchester United football manager Sir Alex Ferguson, he said one of the greatest transitions to him becoming one of the most successful managers of all time was when his

21. Dave Murphy, "Leadership Is Responsibility, Not Power," *Insights* (May 1, 2009), https://www.gsb.stanford.edu/insights/leadership-responsibility-not-power.

assistant coach at Aberdeen, Archie Knox, sat him down and told him that he needed to be less involved in running the daily training sessions.[22] Archie thought Alex was too involved with managing the training sessions and that he was neglecting his duties as the leader. Archie's suggestion was for Alex to let him run the session and to spend more time in observation so then he could give better feedback to his players. Alex could see more and then understand his players better and even spend more individual time with players as he walked around observing. He could then give better evaluations and, more importantly, lead. To his credit, Alex took his assistant's suggestion, and he was eventually knighted by the queen of England and became one of the most successful managers in the history of world soccer. He said, "It was the most important decision I ever made about the way I managed and led."

How do we do that as coaches? We need to present a clear picture to our staff and players of their roles in the organization. What are they responsible for on and off the pitch? What are their duties? What are your expectations? Convey to them that they have responsibilities in their roles and ask them if they are ready to accept ownership of those responsibilities. If they accept the roles and responsibilities, then keep them accountable. The role of the coach is to remind everyone on the team of their responsibilities and to revisit them if they are neglectful or aren't executing properly or being efficient.

ESTABLISHING A STANDARD

I find it is easier to communicate responsibilities when you have a set standard within your organization. For example, within our team and our school we have a standard of **Excellence in Everything**. I think it's the first thing you see when you visit The King's Academy website.[23] Excellence is a difficult thing to obtain, but it's amazing how much you can accomplish when you set excellence as your standard.

I set the standard for my team as the "relentless pursuit of excellence." We set rules and minimum benchmarks that are clearly stated at the beginning of the season. I know our athletic director, Dr. Chris Hobbs, has gone as far as to have his players sign a contract accepting the standard. Some programs ask the parents and their players to sign a standards-

22. Alex Ferguson and Michael Moritz, *Leading* (New York: Hachette Books, 2015).
23. The King's Academy, accessed July 1, 2019, https://www.tka.net/.

based contract outlining the basic responsibilities of the student-athlete and the parent. Professional sports teams do the same with players. You may put it in a manual or on posters on the wall. Whatever you do, set a standard, even if it's minimal at first. Do what you can manage, and reevaluate later. It's an easy way to make it clear for everyone, and it makes future conversations around responsibilities a little easier.

I will add this: The lower the standard, the lower the level of immediate responsibility assumed and the higher the degree of accountability needed by the coach. A high standard will have other players and coaches holding each other accountable and will take some of the burden off you as the head coach.

Now to be clear, **standards** are not the same as **rules**. A standard is defined as a level of quality or attainment or as an image of measurement or evaluation. Rules are the restrictions and regulatory boundaries we set. Your standard is the measuring stick of the quality of the environment, performance, energy, effort, and character of your players and team, just to name a few attributes. A standard is something to be obtained. A goal for which to strive. It allows for creativity and flexibility in the pursuit of it. A standard when properly set is empowering, not restrictive. As a coach, it's much easier for me to just point to the standard when evaluating the team's or player's effort or performance. It pretty much speaks for itself.

"When we treat people merely as they are, they will remain as they are. When we treat them as if they were what they should be, they will become what they should be." (Thomas S. Monson)

Your players made an investment and accepted some ownership; now give them some responsibility. Set a standard, and present a clear picture of the role. Explain the job duties. Convey your expectations of them in that role, and ask them if they are ready to accept ownership of those responsibilities. Confirm their commitment.

RESPONSE-ABILITY

Another way I think we have to look at responsibility in leadership is by breaking the word out into **response** and **ability**. How do we respond to certain situations? Response-ability is a choice and an action. It forces us to respond to the situation and make a decision. How we respond to victory or adversity determines our future. Some people experience failure and decide to lower their expectations of their team, business, or life. Some people experience victory and then rest on their laurels. For others, their response narrows their focus and allows them to increase their performance.

National Football League coach Bill Belichick and quarterback Tom Brady won their first Super Bowl in 2002 with the New England Patriots, in Tom Brady's second season. As famously known, Tom Brady was a sixth round NFL draft pick and the backup quarterback when the season started. Only an injury to Drew Bledsoe thrust him into the starting role. Over the next 17 years, the Patriots led by this duo would return to the Super Bowl eight more times and win five additional Super Bowl titles, arguably cementing them as the best coach and quarterback in NFL history. During that timeframe no other team has won more than two Super Bowls. Brady and Belichick became even more driven to win after their first Super Bowl victory.

Response-ability is extremely important in communication within the team and with players. As coaches we need to help players understand that they are also responsible for what and how they say things to other players on the team and to the opponents. Maybe more importantly, they also need to be responsible for fully listening to coaches and teammates and for how they hear what's being communicated to them.

In *The Messiah Method*, the author shares a great principle used by the Messiah teams that I've tried to adopt with our team.[24] In communication with teammates, "mean no offense and take no offense." Meaning that we are all on the same team and that our speech to each other should be to encourage, improve, and discuss solutions. As coaches and players, we have to be open to receiving feedback on our performances without offense, which can sometimes be hard because we all have an ego and the delivery can sometimes feel harsh. As coaches and players, we have to be tactful with our delivery of feedback and try not to offend. If we take "mean no offense, take no offense" to heart and our ultimate heart is for our teammates and team goals, our response-ability becomes much easier.

---

24. Michael Zigarelli, *The Messiah Method* (Maitland: Xulon Press, 2011).

COACHES' BOX: WHO IS JERRY NORMAN?

Pretty much every coach knows the name John Wooden. But you may have never heard the name Jerry Norman. Interestingly enough, some of the credit for Coach John Wooden's eventual success at UCLA goes to his assistant coach Jerry Norman, who they say persuaded Coach Wooden that the team's small-sized players and fast-paced offense would be complemented by the adoption of a zone press defense. UCLA went on to have its first undefeated season and win the first of Coach John Wooden's and UCLA's 10 NCAA men's basketball championships. The ability to delegate and listen to others are just two character traits that allowed coach John Wooden to become one of the greatest coaches of all time.

VIRGINIA MEN'S BASKETBALL

Recently, the University of Virginia men's basketball team turned around in the most remarkable redemption in college sports, according to most sportswriters, by winning the NCAA men's basketball national championship for the first time in school history in their first appearance in the finals. The reason sportswriters used the word "redemption" was because the team's fall from the tournament the year before had been so tragic and surprising. UVA had never won a NCAA men's basketball championship, even though they showed tons of promise. They were often criticized for never living up to the potential of their team and never making it to the finals. They had won the ACC championship in four of the last six seasons and entered that year's tournament as the #1 overall ranked seed before a devastating loss to a #16 seed knocked them out of the tournament. The embarrassing exit from the tournament came with a lot of criticism but also allowed the head coach and his players some time to reflect. Coach Tony Bennett stated,

> "I'm thankful in a way for what happened because it did, it drew me closer, most importantly, to my faith in the Lord, drew me closer to my wife and children, just because you realize what's unconditional. In those spots when the world's telling you you're

Joby Slay

a failure, you're a loser, and you're the worst thing going and all that stuff, you say, 'OK, what really matters?' And it pushed me to that in a way."[25]

One of the articles I came across online after their victory was from Rob Dauster on NBCsports.com in a college basketball talk blog. The title of the article was "What Got You Here Won't Get You There: The inside story of how UMBC changed Virginia."[26] UMBC was the #16 seed team that embarrassed Bennett and his team the previous year. Dauster pointed out that Virginia head basketball coach Tony Bennett had been steadfast in a style of play that had proven very successful for him. The loss to UMBC forced him to reevaluate the style that had made him so successful.

Jim Collins many years earlier coined a statement that I think captures this moment of reflection for Bennett: "The Good is the enemy of the Great."[27] Bennett's struggle was similar to what my team faced this year during our high school soccer regular season. If Bennett's team had not been knocked out of the tournament in such a devastating way, they probably would have thought they were okay. Just another normal close loss to a good team. Just as, if we had won the close games we dropped in the first half of our season, we may very well have been sitting at 7–3 or even at .500. We may have thought we were okay and good enough to win our district and been reluctant to change what was working. The blessing was in the loss. The ability to respond to the loss and seek to improve and change was a responsibility Bennett and players needed to assume.

Within days, Bennett began the process with his team of responding to the loss. Dauster writes that Bennett reached out to ask for help from a New Zealand basketball player named Kirk Penney, who had played for

25. George Schroeder, "Virginia, Tony Bennett Make NCAA National Championship a Father and Son Reunion," *USA Today Sports* (April 9, 2019), https://www.msn.com/en-us/kids/other/virginia-tony-bennett-make-ncaa-national-championship-a-father-and-son-reunion/ar-BBVKINR?li=BBnb7Kz.
26. Rob Dauster, "What Got You Here Won't Get You There: The inside story of how UMBC changed Virginia," *NBC Sports* (April 8, 2019), https://collegebasketball.nbcsports.com/2019/04/08/what-got-you-here-wont-get-you-there-the-inside-story-of-how-umbc-changed-virginia/.
27. Jim Collins, *Good To Great* (New York: Harper Business, 2001).

Bennett at Wisconsin and then played professionally all over the world. Coach Bennett was humble enough to ask for help. Penney visited with Bennett over the summer and helped him install a new system. UVA went on to post a 35–3 record during the season after reinventing his system. The "response-ability" of Bennett and his players led them to the pinnacle of college basketball.

SCOUTING REPORT LESSONS

▶ Leaders grant responsibility to others.

▶ Leaders understand how to convey responsibility clearly to their players.

▶ Leaders set a standard that everyone on the team can hold each other accountable to.

▶ Leaders have a strong response-ability in pivotal situations.

▶ Leaders ask for help, listen, and share decision-making responsibilities with others.

▶ Leaders can learn from the examples of the coaches I share in this chapter: Manchester United manager Sir Alex Ferguson; University of Virginia's 2019 NCAA Men's Basketball National Championship head coach Tony Bennett; and the all-time winningest collegiate men's basketball coach, John Wooden. Surround yourself with others who aren't afraid to remind you of your responsibility.

COACHES' BOX: DELEGATING

I know many coaches are asking, How do I delegate some responsibilities to others if I don't have others around me? You say, "I coach 10- to 12-year-old kids and have no assistants." I get it. I've struggled with it myself. I know it can be difficult, but I'm going to make this statement to you. It is **your** responsibility as the head coach to find help. If you try to do everything yourself, the team will suffer, and so will you. Do yourself a favor and **ask** for help. I had to ask for help with this project. Get a team mom or dad or grandparent to help with communicating and scheduling. Ask another parent, grandparent, or friend if they want to help you coach. You'll be surprised once you put it out there how many people might be willing to step up and help. Give them the opportunity to help you. Sometimes people are just waiting for someone to ask.

CHAPTER SEVEN
RESPECT

"Nobody cares how much you know, until they know how much you care." (Attributed to Theodore Roosevelt)

Without respect, you have nothing.

In 2005, when the idea was first formulated in my mind for the *GET MOR³EE* acronym, the "R" originally represented just responsibility. As I thought about it further, I realized that the desire to have greater responsibility alone was not enough for a person to be highly motivated. *Why would any human being want just more responsibility?* I thought. I mean, that sounds like work. That means I have to be accountable for something or to someone. I'm responsible, which means that if I fail at this then there possibly are negative repercussions. Well, then, why would I want that responsibility? Why am I and why are others motivated to take on responsibility? What are the intangible and tangible reasons?

And the answer came to me, summed up in these two words: respect and rewards. I realized in my own life and by observing life around me that a person's attraction to greater responsibility was deeply motivated by the desire for greater respect and rewards. I'm willing to accept the risk that comes with responsibility because of the promise of greater respect and rewards.

Respect is having a feeling of deep admiration for someone or something. So we accept the responsibility for a task or role because we have an admiration for the leader or someone else who represents that position. For a public service person or someone serving in our military, maybe it's a deep respect for the flag, the country, or the people serving alongside you. Maybe you admire the role you are in and feel it's your duty to respect those under your command by serving them well. Maybe there is a higher calling on your life and you take on the responsibility of answering that call because of the respect you have for the one who is calling you.

Some people are motivated to take on a responsibility because they want to earn the admiration of others or they need the admiration that comes from a title. Some people are fulfilled and motivated by the admiration that comes from elevation of position or status, so they are willing to accept the responsibility that comes with that role in order to get that respect. I might desire the respect of people from accomplishing something considered great in their eyes, like winning some kind of competition or award or receiving fame.

Whether it's the type of respect a person feels internally that's being given or respect that one desires to receive, as coaches we must recognize that both are strong motivators of people's intentions and both are useful for getting more out of people.

Respect is also a due regard for the feelings, wishes, rights, or traditions of others. People might say they take on a responsibility because it's been a tradition in their family. For some people, respect may be a cultural responsibility. For others, respect for the hierarchy of the organization may dictate their responsibilities. They may be willing to do something because someone they respect asked them. Players may show respect simply because they are motivated by the feelings, wishes, rights, and traditions of others.

Another aspect of respect is to agree to recognize or abide by something. My wife tends to be a rule follower. If the sign at the pool says "Open Dawn to Dusk," then at sundown we've got to go before the FBI and SWAT teams swoop in to get us out. Me, I might be a little more like *This hot tub is nice and it's not dusk in Singapore. Which dusk are they talking about? It's not very clear.*

In any case, there are rules and standards out there, and we all have our level of respect for the differing principles, laws, and rules. The respect level we have for certain rules, people, or things leads us to agree to recognize and abide by them. One of the things I learned in my research that I had not fully recognized before is that respect is a choice. Respect motivates us to make a decision. Respect motivates our actions and our commitment.

ASSETS OR TOOLS

Today we see countless stories coming out about very successful people, coaches, businesspeople, and politicians who achieved great results in life, got the trophies, made the money, won the race, built the business empire, but left a wake of destruction—tons of broken people as a result of their actions. I think it's because they look at people as tools, not assets. Tools have limited value. They are valuable for the job or moment, and with a tool you're just looking to work it hard and get as much out of it as you can, and the tool gets nothing back. It's just used and worked until it either breaks or is no longer needed.

An asset has value and creates a return. You invest time and resources into managing an asset and look to create greater value over time so the asset can produce a greater return. Ask yourself: Do I look at people as an asset or a tool? Do I value the people around me? Do I value the people I lead? Do I respect their talents and contributions to the organization? If you don't offer respect to the person first, regardless of the job and everything else, you will never be able to get more and create sustainable growth and empowerment in your organization with the people under your leadership.

THE GET MOR³EE CYCLE OF SUSTAINABLE GROWTH AND EMPOWERMENT

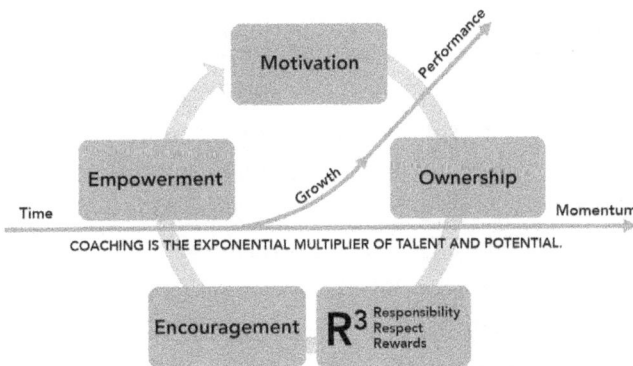

Diagram 2: The GET MOR³EE Formula Cycle

GET MOR³EE is a formula for creating sustained growth in the people you are leading, but if you don't value them, you will just break them rather than create value in them. Instead of a cycle of **motivation →**

ownership → **responsibility, respect, rewards** → **encouragement** → **empowerment = momentum**, your cycle will become start → push → break → stop → remove → replace → start over. It's very hard to build anything of great value when you are constantly destroying, stopping to clean up and carry stuff out to the dumpster, and expending your resources to replace things.

> *"You don't get the best out of people by hitting them with an iron rod. You do so by gaining their respect, getting them accustomed to triumphs and convincing them that they are capable of improving their performance."* (Sir Alex Ferguson)[28]

"DO YOU VALUE PEOPLE?"

I asked this question of a colleague one day many years ago when we were having a discussion about the people who worked for us. We were discussing developing, building, and motivating five or so people, and as we were discussing the process, I said, "Let me ask you a question: Do you value these people?" I could see immediately the change in the expression on this person's face. My colleague was taken aback a little bit, and I could see the wheels start turning as my colleague pondered the question and maybe was a little surprised about the immediate thoughts that came to mind. After more than a few seconds, my colleague responded with "No, I don't."

Right at that moment I knew that we had an issue that would be potentially detrimental to our company and a stumbling block to moving forward if there was no way for this person to value the people we were managing. I felt right then that we would have a hard time growing and developing these people or anyone else we brought into the company the way we said we wanted to if we didn't respect them.

Now I don't think my colleague was admitting a complete lack of concern for people but in this instance was admitting a lack of **respect** for the unique talents or abilities that the individuals contributed to the organization. I think we have many leaders out there who think the same way. They have a good heart, are good people, and are very talented, but they evaluate people through the lens of thinking that if people don't have the same abilities as them and are not at their level or don't speak or

28. Alex Ferguson and Michael Moritz, *Leading* (New York: Hachette Books, 2015), 118.

talk or dress the same as them, then they are inadequate or incapable. I've heard many leaders make the statement "Imagine what I could do if only I had a dozen carbon copies of myself!" The breakthrough moment for many leaders comes in the realization that their people don't need to be just like them, and you probably don't want them to be, in order for them to focus in and do the job and role they were hired to do.

RESPECTING DIFFERING TALENTS

I believe that the beauty of innovation and creativity comes not from having a dozen of the same like-minded, same-skilled clones of people in an organization but from the chaos and friction from ideas, people, and things sometimes breaking and banging into one another—leading everyone to discover what is truly innovative and what really works.

One of the things I love about sports and about coaching is seeing how the different personalities and skill sets come together within the team. The playing field can look like an absolute mess at times. Nothing seems to go right, and then that same group of people when properly motivated and organized can become a powerful machine of endless possibilities. The field of competition is like a crucible that burns off the impurities, molding and forming teams and players. It either burns them up or strengthens their mettle.

Now if you are the coach, entrepreneur, idea person, creator, or inventor, then all the people who work for you do not have to be "on your level" to provide value and for you to value them. Do you value them as individuals? Do you respect them? If you can't value and respect individuals, then you are going to have a hard time leading them and developing them. You can motivate them and push them for a little while and get results, but it's going to be short-lived. You are going to have a lot of turnover, and you are going to have to repeat the cycle of starting over, pushing, losing the person, repeat. It's an exhausting process, and you are never getting the most or getting more out of those people. I've heard it said that the simple loss of a manager or leader within an organization can set a company back six months or more! The people in your organization don't have time to develop and grow into leaders. They have a more difficult time feeling encouraged to grow on their own and grow others in your organization. They never reach empowerment.

WHERE POWER COMES FROM

I think sometimes as leaders we want to be a leader because we want people to serve us instead of being in a servant leadership role. Some people in leadership positions have a need to serve their egos, and they crave recognition or admiration and want people to respect them. They desire to have people looking to them as leaders and maybe worshipping them as the leader because they have some authority or power over other people that they've obtained from their title, role, or position.

Now I believe that even if coaches have that type of mentality, the GET MOR^{3}EE formula can help them with connecting and respecting the people around them while still maybe satisfying their ego and allowing the individuals under their purview to flourish, grow, and develop.

Something I say to myself to help keep my ego in check is **"Power comes from the vision, not the volume."**

What I mean by that statement is that power doesn't come from being louder than everyone else or by overwhelming them with the volume of your words. The true show of someone's leadership and authority is that he or she can grant power to another person. When you are really able to instill into people the integrity of your position, leadership, and authority is when you are able to give power and empower the other people around you. If you are struggling with this, then keep reading! The GET MOR^{3}EE formula will help you discover that ability within you by giving you the process and accountability that you can rely on.

MODELING RESPECT

One of the most effective ways for a coach to teach the concept of respect to players is to model it. Respect can be difficult to communicate to your players in a meaningful way. The best visual of what respect actually is will come from them watching you. How do you respond to those in authority above you? Establish with your team that you follow the chain of command in your organization. Let them know that some of the decisions you make are in adherence to directives from your superiors.

One of our assistant coaches for the boys' soccer team I coach was promoted to assistant athletic director this past year. He is almost 20 years my junior in age and now technically my boss. When he went into this role, I understood that there are times when he is no longer an assistant coach, and I need to relegate my authority and defer decision-making in some areas to his position. When he is wearing his assistant coach hat and supporting me, he does a great job of flipping roles and following my lead and carrying out my directives. We are both modeling respect to our players for the positions of authority.

My friend Andrew Mehalko provided this description of a relationship full of respect: Many people think of respect as a 50/50 relationship where both parties have an equal 50 percent share in the relationship; the truth is that the most productive relationships modeling the highest level of respect are where both parties assume 100 percent responsibility for the relationship.

Coaches, how are you communicating your respect for others? When an authority figure is not in your presence, do you speak disrespectfully about them in front of your team? Are you gossiping about parents or other coaches? Do you speak negatively to or about a player in front of other players? Do you constantly chide players for their play in front of others or lay blame solely on their name for a negative result? If you do, then you are granting permission to other players to do the same thing to that person and modeling a disrespectful attitude to your team. It starts with you, Coach. Model edifying communication within your team. Be consistent. Quickly limit any undesirable speech or self-talk within the team. You get to establish the language your team speaks. If you don't like it, change it. It's within your power.

COACHES' BOX: CLEAR COMMUNICATION

"The single biggest problem in communication is the illusion that it has taken place." (Attributed to George Bernard Shaw)

Some of the challenges of respect and communication we face within our teams are a result of our assumption that our players know or should know what we want of them. I've made this mistake many times in my own coaching. Lack of preparation or sheer laziness on my part has caused major grief or unnecessary friction within our team when player responsibilities and my vision for the team have not been communicated clearly. I make it a practice now to put the most important messages on paper and deliver them to the team or individuals face-to-face. I want to limit any confusion and assumptions, and that can best be done when discussions and questions are fostered in an in-person setting. Body language, voice inflection, and pace of speech—all of which can influence the urgency and importance of your message—can get lost in text messages, email, or phone calls.

As coaches, our reliance on others to communicate our messages is a massive error in judgment on our part. Take control of the narrative of your team, or someone else will. The following are the four rules of communication I follow with my teams:

1. COMMUNICATE OFTEN.
2. BE CLEAR.
3. BE CONCISE.
4. BE CONSISTENT.

HOW DOES RESPECT RELATE TO THE TEAM?

My high school football coach, Coach Dave Vercillo, once gave us this analogy to describe the guys he wanted on the team with him: If cornered in a dark alley by a group of thugs and backed against a wall, he wanted the guys who would stick and fight with him and not try to run away when the fight started.

Each season always presents its own unique set of challenges. A team that has mutual respect for one another and the needs of the individual always has an easier time navigating the trials and has a better chance of overcoming the obstacles to victory. I want my players to have individual goals. One of my requests of them at the start of the season is to set individual goals along with their team goals, and I follow up throughout the season to see how they are doing on those goals. I know that is one of the many reasons we were successful this past season in winning the district championship. When we knew we had to change and we made that commitment as a team, the players **all** relegated their personal ambitions below the overall success of the team. When I later asked them about their individual goals, it was almost as if they no longer had any further personal ambition other than achieving the team goal. Their personal goal had become the success of the team.

THE SHOELACE

In our regional quarterfinal game of the state playoff series, our leading offensive player, Jared Brown, broke a shoelace midway through the second half. It was a tight 0–0 game. We substituted another player in for him but desperately wanted to get our leading goal scorer back on the field for the remaining minutes of the game. As we fished around for a shoelace that would fit this type of shoe, one of our juniors, Matias Uribe, sat down on the ground and started removing his shoelace. He said, "I got it, Coach. I'll give him mine." What was happening in that moment was that Matias realized the importance of the situation and at the same time gave up any chance of going into the game by giving up his shoe. It's a shining example of what mutual respect looks like within a team because mutual respect requires the sacrifice of the individual's desires to the desires of the collective.

In that moment, it seemed as if a team of surgeons quickly gathered to remove the shoelaces from both players' shoes, as players and assistant coaches jumped into action. They laced Jared up, and he was ready to go, and we got him back on the field. Within a few minutes, Jared sent the pass through that was the game-winning assist on what was a miraculous goal. The King's Academy boys' soccer team advanced to the Florida State Series boys' soccer regional semifinal playoff game for only the second time in school history.

SCOUTING REPORT LESSONS

▶ Without respect you have nothing.
▶ Respect is a choice.
▶ Respect is a powerful motivator.
▶ We give respect out of duty, tradition, moral obligation, admiration, and law.
▶ Respect is also a value we place on others.
▶ The coach or leader must offer his or her people respect first if he or she ever expects to be able to successfully empower them.

▶ *Power comes from the vision, not the volume.*

▶ A successful team always shares deep mutual respect for one another.

CHAPTER EIGHT
REWARDS

"The price of victory is high but so are the rewards." (Attributed to Coach Paul Bear Bryan, who coached the University of Alabama to six college football national championships)

One of my favorite shows on television over the past several years has been *The Curse of Oak Island,* airing on the History channel. In January of 1965, an article was published in *Reader's Digest* about a mysterious treasure on Oak Island in the Canadian province of Nova Scotia.[29] A man named Dan Blankenship read this article, along with many others, and it compelled him to leave everything he knew and move to the island with his family and commit his life to finding this treasure. Around that same time, two brothers, Rick and Marty Lagina, read the same *Reader's Digest* article as children, and the story immediately captured their imagination, so much so that it led them to the island 50 years later to partner with the same Dan Blankenship, and now they are working to fulfill this dream they've had since childhood to find buried treasure and solve the 220-year-old Oak Island mystery.[30]

I'll provide a little backstory on this treasure hunt. In 1795, a teenager, Daniel McGinnis, saw some lights coming from an island and upon investigating reportedly found a disturbed area in the ground. McGinnis and two friends, after some digging, were said to have found some treasure chests. He returned years later to the same spot with more

---

29. David MacDonald, "Oak Island's Mysterious 'Money Pit,'" *Reader's Digest* (January 1965), http://www.oakislandbook.com/wp-content/uploads/Readers-Digest-January-1965-OakIslandsMysteriousMoneyPit.pdf.

30. The story of the expeditions to Oak Island is chronicled in the recent History Canada production *The Curse of Oak Island.* See https://www.history.com/shows/the-curse-of-oak-island/about.

help and continued to dig 90 feet underground, pursuing more treasure. The hole they were in was then flooded by seawater, from booby traps, it's theorized. People, including the 32nd president of the United States, Franklin Delano Roosevelt, have been coming to the island ever since, investing their lives and their savings to find this treasure. Still, more than 220 years later, they've yet to find it, but they keep coming back, sinking millions of dollars into the search.

This mysterious treasure is theorized to be many things. Some think it could be hidden caches of pirate treasure around the island. Some think it could be the lost riches of King Solomon's temple and the ark of the covenant placed by the Knights Templar for safekeeping. A recent theorist spoke of a treasure possibly valued at a half-billion dollars hidden on Oak Island! And so far, they have made some fascinating finds over the years. Pieces of gold. Spanish and European coins from the 1700s. Gems and strange weapons theorized to be from Roman times. A lead cross from the 14th century with lead traced back to mines in Europe. Bone fragments belonging to two different people of European and Middle Eastern descent excavated from 160 feet underground, along with leather book binding and parchment from the same hole thought to also be from the 1500s to 1600s.

What are human bones of Europeans from five centuries ago doing 160 feet underground on this island in North America? And why did someone hundreds of years ago go through so much trouble to dig so far underground and build booby traps? What were they hiding? What were they trying to protect? Six people have died trying to find this treasure, and countless others have invested millions to no avail. Why do they continue to return? What is so fascinating about this story? Why do I keep watching? I'll tell you! It's the lure and possibility of receiving an amazing reward. Not just a monetary reward, but also the intellectual reward of solving this mystery!

The larger and more valuable I perceive the reward to be, the greater my interest.

MONEY

Rewards seemingly should be the easiest of the properties in the GET MOR³EE formula to understand and explain. Money is probably the one reward that most readily comes to mind in our society. The employee-employer relationship is built upon the understanding that as an employee I am committing my time for a monetary reward to be received from the employer. Some relationships are a standard time-for-money reward. Others are a result-based monetary award, like a salesperson might receive, and some are a hybrid. I take on this responsibility, and you pay me. This is my reward for accepting the responsibility. As we discussed earlier, people will typically expect a greater reward for taking on more responsibility. Others, like in the Oak Island treasure example, make a huge investment of time, effort, and money motivated by the search for a greater reward.

THE JUICE BOX AND THE TROPHY

In athletics, the majority of us are playing for a trophy or some other symbol of being victorious. This is our reward for winning the final game. In youth sports, a reward for playing might be a juice box and a snack! In high school sports, a reward might be making the varsity team or winning a district championship. In college athletics, receiving a scholarship is one reward. Beyond that, I may take on the responsibility that comes with pursuing the life of a professional athlete for the monetary reward, notoriety, or a championship title and a trophy or other symbol of my accomplishment. I also receive the ability to say I was best in the state, nation, or world at something for one moment in time.

Rewards are a powerful motivator, and many times the perceived rewards are enough to get a person engaged to pursue a relationship with you, your company, or your team. I would think that most of the time those first perceived rewards have a physical presence because you can touch them and they are easy to see and trade. Like money or a trophy—those are tangible rewards. Intangible rewards, those rewards that we can't really touch and don't have a physical form but we know are there all the same, can be a more powerful motivator than any amount of money or item. As the coach and leader, it's your job to present to your team the possible rewards for assuming responsibility and respecting the process and people around you.

What are the rewards, and can you paint a clear picture for the people on your team?

COACH RONNIE LEE

Here is an example of how painting a clear picture for your team can prove powerful in the advancement of your own coaching career.

I met Coach Ronnie Lee during my first season of coaching at The King's Academy. He was new to the school as well and a PE teacher and defensive coordinator for the Lions football team. Coach Lee, as he's referred to around campus, came to The King's Academy with a couple of decades of coaching experience in the college game. In the fall of 2018, with Coach Lee as the defensive coordinator, he and head coach Keith Allen overcame all obstacles to take The King's Academy to the state championship game. At the same time, Coach Lee was invited to coach in the startup Alliance of American Football professional league by famed coach Dennis Erickson, who coached the Miami Hurricanes to the 1989 Collegiate National Championship, where Coach Lee was a graduate assistant. Coach Lee took the opportunity to reunite with Coach Erickson as the defensive backs coach for the Salt Lake City Stallions. After the Stallions' first game of the season, I heard that Coach Lee was being promoted to defensive coordinator. I ran into Coach Lee's wife at church a few weeks later, and she explained to me what happened and one of the reasons Coach Lee thinks he was promoted to defensive coordinator.

She explained that the general manager would frequently sit in on the coaches' different meetings, whether a larger team meeting or just with the position groups. He noticed that Coach Lee's teaching style was different than many of the other, also very experienced, coaches. Coach Lee was providing his players with many visuals. He was helping them envision how the little things they did were impactful to the outcome of the game. He was painting them a picture! The general manager stated to Coach Lee that in all his experience he had never seen anyone coach this way with professionals, and Coach Lee thinks that was one of the reasons the GM promoted him to defensive coordinator.

I was able to catch up with Coach Lee about a month later to ask him about the experience. He credited coming to The King's Academy to coach high school for those few years as making him a better coach. With collegiate and professional players, the coaches many times just talk to the players, and because they are at a high level, the coaches assume the players know or should know what is being explained to them.

He also said that he had to create the proper teaching environment. Instead of just being in a room watching film and discussing the concepts with guys jotting notes in playbooks sitting in their laps, Coach Lee went about creating a classroom environment, a place most people would associate as a space for learning. He brought in tables so the players had a proper writing station for taking notes and whiteboards to write out the day's training plan and create visuals. The other position coaches began to do the same. Coach Lee wanted an environment where the players also felt comfortable dialoguing and providing feedback. He said coaching the high school kids and assuming they didn't know made him a better coach because at the high school level he needed to spend time with every position group. He wasn't just coaching defensive backs anymore. He needed to paint the picture for all the position groups and help them connect the dots in the most basic of ways for understanding how their role affected all the other defensive players. To be successful, Coach Lee had to find ways to show these boys how their assignments impacted the overall defensive scheme. And he carried this process with him to the professional level.

Coach Lee said one of the things he became so accustomed to at the college and high school level was the many walkthroughs he would do with his teams, but at the professional level he found that walkthroughs didn't seem to be a priority. When he took over as defensive coordinator, he instituted more walkthroughs. Coach Lee explained that all these players had grown up training in a similar way. Why would you stop doing what has been so effective for their learning just because they are now professionals? He said that knowing and understanding your players are massively important. "I can only keep DBs [defensive backs] in a classroom for about twenty to thirty minutes, and then they started getting antsy and distracted," he explained. "I need to get them up moving around and out on the field." Coach Lee was implementing the old teaching philosophy of teach, model, and demonstrate.

1. Teach: first, I'm going to tell you what I want you to do and know.
2. Model: second, I'm going to show you what I want you to do and know.
3. Demonstrate: last, you are going to demonstrate some proficiency to me that demonstrates that you can perform what I just taught and modeled to you.

Here is why this story is so valuable to all of us as coaches: painting the picture was effective in increasing player performance. Coach Lee professed that this practice raised the level of his coaching acumen. The opportunity to practice this has opened up many other potential opportunities for him. Players improved. Performance improved. Results improved. And people noticed.

PAINT THE PICTURE; CONNECT THE REWARDS

Can you paint the picture of how ownership, responsibility, and respect connect with the potential rewards your players can receive? Can you create an image of intangible rewards connected to a physical reward for the people around you?

For example, a trophy might say "First Place" on it, but it represents much more than that. It represents that you were the team that was best able to come together and work together to accomplish more than anyone else that season by your collective efforts and commitment. You will forever be able to call yourselves the champions. The power of envisioning "champion" being connected to your player's name forever can be a powerful motivator, and I can use the physical trophy as that reminder.

This season our team was celebrated as having more success than any other team in our area, winning the district championship. Our team was rewarded with a district championship trophy. The players received district championship T-shirts and patches. A few of them received All-County First Team, Second Team, or Honorable Mention recognition. As a byproduct, a reward for me, being the head coach of the team, was that I was voted boys' soccer Coach of the Year. As a coaching staff, we painted the picture and tied all those possible individual and team rewards together and allowed it to be a powerful motivator for our team.

Tangible rewards are again pretty easy to see. If you do this, you win this plaque. Pretty much every league and team has an award for the top-scoring player during a season. If I'm the top scorer, I may receive an Offensive Player of the Year plaque or the Offensive MVP trophy or the title Scoring Champion. If I establish myself as a leader within the team, I may get to wear the captain's armband, and this is also an example of a tangible reward that could be motivated and multiplied with responsibility and respect.

Desired intangible rewards can be harder to see and discover in people but just as easy to describe. An intangible reward for student athletes might be the pride of playing for their school. It may just be the desire to grow or accomplish something. There is usually some internal reward that motivates your athletes. It could be personal satisfaction or simply love of the activity.

Discovering and mining these motivations out of your players is like discovering a gold mine or rich oil field. Identifying the motivations of your players and the rewards they desire will prove massively valuable to the success you create with your team.

INDIVIDUAL REWARDS AND TEAM REWARDS

Whether it's a tangible or intangible reward, you're celebrating the result of your players accomplishing something you asked them to do. The accomplishment had value for you, the individual, the company, and the team. It's not always obvious what is a greater motivator for an individual, and this comes back to knowing your people. It may not be getting a plaque at the end of the season that says MVP. We think everyone wants that, but maybe they don't. You don't have to be a shrink and have a psychology degree, but you need to be willing to spend time with them, observe, and be willing to ask them questions and listen. Some people don't care about the individual awards and put team accomplishments above all else. That is their reward, so as a coach you have to be careful about focusing on their individual results. You may be able to get more out of them, and they will work harder when focused on how doing a task well or practicing harder benefits the team.

THE AGENT OF THE YEAR AWARD

In the book *First, Break All the Rules*, Marcus Buckingham and Curt Coffman share a story of a manager and a salesman that I think illustrates this point well.[31] In summary, a top-producing sales agent expressed to his manager that he would rather not receive another meaningless plaque for his recognition as Agent of the Year again. If the manager wanted to recognize him, the salesman said he would prefer something a little more meaningful to him. The manager thought he knew better and at

---

31. Marcus Buckingham and Curt Coffman, *First, Break All The Rules* (New York: Simon and Schuster, 1999).

the awards banquet proceeded to try to honor the salesman with another plaque. It was a disaster. The salesman walked off the stage without the plaque and vowed to quit the company.

The manager talked to the salesman's colleagues to see if there was any way he could salvage the situation. During this process, he found out that the salesman absolutely adored his two daughters. Talked about them all the time. The manager called the salesman's wife, and they came up with an idea. A couple of weeks later, they called a meeting at the company and presented the salesman with a beautiful portrait they had commissioned of his two daughters. They had it fitted into a frame that was embossed with his Agent of the Year plaque. The salesman cried. I'm sure at different times in his career the salesman was motivated by money or maybe even to be the number one salesperson. He had already several times over received his reward for his sales responsibilities and recognition for being the number one salesperson. Once the manager was able to tie what really mattered to the salesman, the intangible love for his daughters, to the tangible reward of the plaque, he was then able to connect the pieces of what truly motivated that salesman.

MY GREATEST TROPHIES

As an athlete and a coach, I've received numerous trophies and awards and won ribbons and medals in high school track and field. I was awarded a Most Valuable Player trophy for my college soccer team and a Goalkeeper of the Year trophy for another league. I won several men's league soccer championships and a couple Babe Ruth Baseball Florida State Championships, and for these I received trophies and such. Hey, I've even won a few scramble event golf trophies, and those were bigger than my MVP trophy! Most recently I received a district championship trophy for the high school boys' soccer team I coach along with a trophy for a Coach of the Year award. For me, the two best rewards I received in athletics include the first championship trophy I received for winning with a top South Florida soccer league alongside all my soccer buddies from college. We had been playing together for almost ten years before we won anything significant, and it meant something personal to me to win with them. The other was the recent district championship as a coach. It was a three-year journey of consecutive district finals appearances before we were able to win it. That journey meant a little more. All of those rewards are great and mean something to me, but they don't compare to a couple of the greatest gifts I ever received.

One gift was from my two-year-old niece and my grandmother at Christmastime a couple of years after my grandfather passed away. It was a little box, and when I opened it I saw two old golf balls. Gran explained that my niece Kaitlynne found these two old golf balls that had belonged to my grandfather when they were walking around the yard one day, and she wanted to give them to Uncle Joby as a Christmas gift. So Gran said she helped Kaitlynne clean them up, find this little box, and wrap them up for me. The thought of them doing that and having those two old golf balls from my grandfather that he'd lost in the yard probably a decade earlier brought me to tears.

The second gift was on my birthday, I think, and from my wife. I have these old medals from my grandfather from when he served in WWII, and they had just been sitting around in a box. Well, without me knowing, she took them and, with the help of a friend, made this little box I could hang on the wall. Through the clear glass, the three medals are displayed along with a picture of my grandfather. It's probably the most meaningful gift I have ever received.

In both those instances, the people who presented those items to me knew that my grandfather was important to me and connected the gifts to my grandfather, and it moved me.

As a coach, I need to understand what my players value so I can tie the rewards to the motivation of my players in helping them get more.

SCOUTING REPORT LESSONS

▶ Rewards are a powerful motivator.

▶ Rewards can be either tangible or intangible.

▶ Connect intangible rewards and tangible rewards together as a powerful motivational image.

▶ Perceived rewards can bring people into a relationship with you.

▶ It's the coach's job to present the possible rewards to the team.

▶ The coach is responsible for painting the picture of how the rewards connect to all the other properties in the GET MOR^{3}EE formula.

▶ People value rewards differently. Understand how to align individual rewards and team rewards.

▶ Intangible rewards like love and loyalty can be more powerful motivators than money or trophies.

▶ As a coach, I need to gain an understanding of what my players value so I can connect the rewards to their motivation.

CHAPTER NINE
ENCOURAGEMENT

In this chapter, I spend a little more time on encouragement than I did with the properties presented in the previous chapters because I believe that your ability to encourage your players is of utmost importance to your effectiveness as a coach.

Encouragement is powerful and necessary for an organization to flourish and grow. Accountability is another form of encouragement. As leaders, we need to recognize the power of routine encouragement, meaning that encouragement needs to be consistent and intentional, and we also need to understand the power of encouragement through accountability.

The following is the one sentence I want you to take away from this chapter if you take away nothing else; it will be your best reminder of how important this property is to your success.

Encouragement is the fuel that leads to empowerment.

THE COACH AS CEO

Michael Zigarelli, PhD, in the book *Ordinary People, Extraordinary Leaders,* makes a reference to the title CEO as Chief Encouragement Officer.[32] As the head coach of a team, you are the CEO: the Chief Encouragement Officer. Dr. Zigarelli makes the connection that leaders who praise frequently are more likely to report being able to get results. I'm going to paraphrase the next sentence to fit the coach: "Encouragement of **players** inspires them to both loyalty and commitment, a tandem that facilitates a **coach's** ability to get results." The coach as CEO is an attitude that both serves the players and maximizes their performance.

---

32. Michael Zigarelli, *Ordinary People, Extraordinary Leaders* (Gainesville: Synergy Publishers, 2002).

Two synonyms I like for encouragement that help explain this CEO idea are "stimulation" and "emboldening." The coach as chief encouragement officer **stimulates** the positive mental outlook of the players, thus **emboldening** their performances.

A coach who does not assume responsibility for his role as CEO may be by default **dissuading** his players from believing in their abilities, thus **hindering** their performance.

LAW OF BELIEF AS ENCOURAGEMENT

Belief from a leader is a huge component of the encouragement piece of the GET MOR³EE formula. When leaders display belief in their players or the people working for them, it gives a higher level of confidence to the people they are leading. Demonstrating the belief that they can achieve what they are setting out to accomplish and the goals that they have set is energizing. Players can sense when they are being filled with falsehoods. They can feel the difference between true belief in them from a coach who cares versus the hollow words of a coach who's just trying to manipulate or pacify them.

Michael Phelps explained in an interview how his coach, Bob Bowman, came to him when he was 11 years old and told him that he believed Michael could qualify for the Olympics in four years.[33] Phelps goes on to say that he wasn't sure what made him trust his coach at 11 years old, but he was looking for someone to express confidence in him, and Coach Bob Bowman did that. So Phelps said okay at 11 years old, and four years later he was competing in his first Olympics at age 15. Immediately after the Olympics, Phelps says, he jumped right back into training, and at their first training session his coach wrote "WR" on top of the training sheet. When Michael asked him why he wrote it, Coach Bowman replied that they were going to break a world record in six months. Michael said okay, and six months later he broke his first world record, and six months after that he broke another and won his first world championship.

---

33. Michael Phelps, "Becoming Michael Phelps: Tony Talks to the Greatest Olympian of All Time About the Art of the Comeback, What It Means to Win, and the Power of Pushing Through," interview by Tony Robbins, *The Tony Robbins Podcast*, podcast audio, April 1, 2019, https://www.tonyrobbins.com/podcasts/becoming-michael-phelps/.

When asked why he trusted his coach, Phelps responded by saying that he didn't really know why, but he knew that Coach Bowman cared and consistently proved the ability to get more out of him. His coach's belief in him may be the most important factor in Michael Phelps developing into the greatest Olympian of all time. Your belief level in your team and the athletes you are coaching may be the most important factor in them discovering their true gifts and talents and reaching a championship level.

Several years ago I coached a group of nine-to-ten-year-old boys to a national championship. It was a 3v3 Disney Youth Soccer National Championship played at ESPN Wide World of Sports in August of 2014. What made us decide to enter such a big tournament in the first place? I believed it would be a good experience and a lot of fun. I also believed that the boys had the ability to compete and maybe something special would happen.

For my son and, I think, four of his friends, the first time they played in a 3v3 tournament together was the month before, and we did okay. The rules for 3v3 are very different, and we only had a couple of weeks to prepare for this national championship tournament. It would be nice to say that I became a 3v3 coaching savant and my tactical strategies led these boys to becoming national champions, but that isn't really how it went.

The first day we played in some qualifying matches, and I can't recall exactly the results of those games, but the boys played fine, and we ended up as the top seed in the Silver Division. As with most great victories, a little bit of luck never hurts, and that was a lucky break for our team. The Silver Division was still a quality group of teams and players.

As play began in the championship rounds, I don't think there was an easy game in the bunch. In fact, I think we may have been down in every game at some point. The biggest challenge for myself and the other dad coaching with me was not the technical or the tactical parts of the game. It wasn't our preparation and training, even though we had had little time to prepare. We prepared the best we could in the time we had. Our biggest challenge—our largest obstacle as coaches—was to constantly encourage the boys to believe they had a chance at victory. And not just before we started the tournament or at the beginning of each day. And not just at the beginning of each game. It was at all those times and multiple times a game. Every game it seemed like we found a way to come back for a late win.

I think it was in the championship game that we were down by a goal with just a few minutes left to play. You could see and feel the worry and uncertainty in the boys. They were tired and hurting and losing. I think a couple of them were actually afraid. We did what I expect many coaches would do at that moment and just told them they could do it. They had the ability to come back and win. "Don't worry about the score; just try your best. Remember what we worked on in training." We did what we had done the whole tournament. We just kept encouraging them to believe in themselves.

I'm not sure if the boys truly had the belief that they could win the tournament or even that game. But, I think they began to believe that we believed in them, and that was enough. Our boys scored two great goals in those last few minutes to come back and win the game. It was a great moment for the boys and possibly an even greater one for us as parents and coaches.

When you genuinely begin to believe that you can get more out of your players than what their "talent" level might suggest, then you have progressed beyond being a trainer and teaching a trade or a skill set to becoming an empowering leader and coach.

COACHES' BOX:
THE DIFFERENCE BETWEEN A TRAINER AND A COACH

Good trainers are valuable. They are akin to a manager in any business. Their main job is to make sure people are doing things right. A coach's role is more akin to that of a leader. The coach's or leader's job is to make sure the team is doing the right things—that the team is on the right path, pursuing the right course of action to obtain the desired results. In training, we can become mesmerized with succeeding at things that do not produce wins on the field or with our players.

The other difference between a trainer and a coach is an adaptation of something I heard Tony Robbins say. A

> trainer gets people to do things while he or she is present. A coach establishes values and a standard so that when he or she is not present the players continue to perform at a higher level.[34]

TALENT DOESN'T ALWAYS WIN

I hear people say that "talent wins every time." Some people in coaching believe that as an absolute. I don't. I've been around athletics for coming up on 40 years. That statement is **absolutely** not true. But, it's easier for some coaches to think that way. As a "talent wins every time" coach, it removes my burden and responsibility to motivate, train, and prepare my team properly. The "talent wins every time" coaches have a ready-made excuse any time their team loses. They just shrug their shoulders and say, "The other team just had more talent." The coach may think this softens the blow for his or her players and makes them feel better. In the long term it doesn't. It's unempowering. It instills in the players that there is absolutely nothing they can do to prepare or improve to win against a team with more "talent." The players then do little to nothing to develop the talent within themselves, never exploring and discovering the full potential of their abilities as players, because their coach has expressed that he or she doesn't believe in their ability. Some players still find a way to grow beyond the coach's indifference, but it takes a very strong self-assurance or someone else helping instill that belief in them.

COACHING IS THE EXPONENTIAL MULTIPLIER OF TALENT AND POTENTIAL

"Exponential multiplier" is a mathematical term that I associate with the value of coaching. People have natural talents and gifts. People have what we call "potential for future development and success," which we infer will come from these talents and gifts or from some unrealized ability. Coaching is the **exponential multiplier** of these talents and potential in people.

I'm not going to attempt to teach you a math equation. Maybe just look up "exponential multiplier," or those of you with math brains may

---

34. Tony Robbins, "Secrets of Peak Performance: What You Can Learn From Tony's Work with the Best Athletes and Coaches in the World," *The Tony Robbins Podcast*, podcast audio, May 1, 2019, https://www.tonyrobbins.com/podcasts/secrets-of-peak-performance/.

have already made the connection. I'll just present a simple diagram to help make the connection between coaching and the exponential growth of a player's performance over time versus the natural development of an uncoached person.

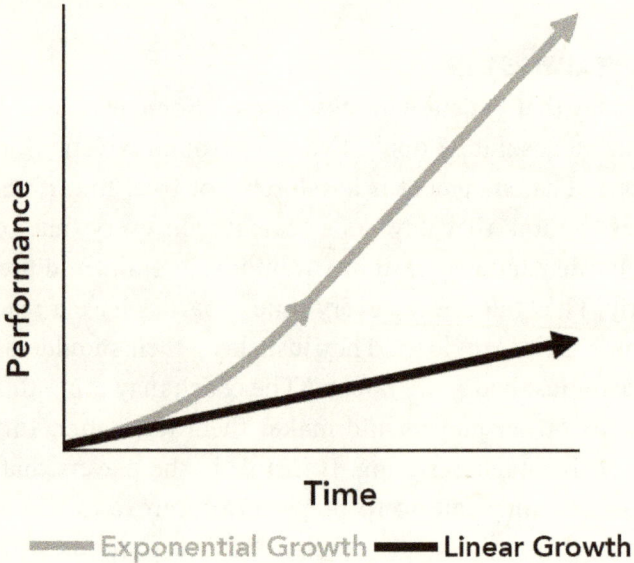

Diagram 3: Exponential Growth

The world shows us that if left alone to develop naturally, people tend to grow in age, size, knowledge, and skills at a reasonable rate of growth over time. On a graph, we may label this **linear** or **natural growth**. Imagine a horizontal line on a graph that is rising gradually into the future. So you have this slightly elevating linear growth line on this graph. Now add in the exponential multiplier of coaching, and your growth rate on your line graph may be rising slightly above your natural growth line. What occurs over time is that the addition of coaching applied to your growth rate results in **exponential growth**. This **coach-led growth** line makes a break-through type move on your graph, climbing sharply upwards at about a 90-degree angle, as the benefits of coaching multiplies the person's talent and potential over time to create massive breakthrough and momentum in development of the person's abilities.

I believe the greatest harvest of the 21st century will be the harvest of human potential. The world's collective level of coaching effectiveness is the exponential multiplier of human potential. The GET MOR³EE formula helps elevate coaching effectiveness.

When you as a coach believe that you are equipped to get more out of your players and make that one of your top priorities, you think and prepare differently. The belief you express in your players instills in them the confidence and motivation to push them beyond where they think they can go. They push themselves to get more!

LAW OF THE LID ON BELIEF

I think the way I am with my players in regards to my belief in them can best be summed up in that I try not to put a lid on them. John Maxwell in his Law of the Lid description states that if the leader is only three out of ten as a leader, then that organization can only grow to or be a level-three type of program.[35] If the leader is a level-eight type of leader, then the organization can perform up to a level-eight type of organization. If a coach or leader has a belief of ten out of ten about what the player or program can accomplish or become, then the team has permission to believe. The coach's belief inspires the level of the team's and players' belief.

Just as Maxwell stated that the leader's level of leadership, the leadership skill, is where the level of the organization is capped, the same can be said of the coach's belief level in his or her players and team. If the coach's belief is capped at a three, then the team and players and everyone else under him or her is capped at the level of the belief of the coach. Consequently, you as a coach are capping yourself in your ability to get more out of your team and players.

I mentioned earlier the need to "begin with the end in mind"—if your belief level is a three, then you are going to build and plan your program to a level three. Then you will be wondering why you can't get to level five or level eight, and you will be disappointed in yourself. If instead you plan to be a ten but only reach level five that season, then you can still feel satisfied that you are building and working towards a ten, and you can build on the season instead of having to tear apart the program to rebuild. Be careful as a coach not to put a lid on the belief you have in your players.

---

35. John C. Maxwell, *The 21 Irrefutable Laws of Leadership* (Nashville: Thomas Nelson, 1998 and 2007). The Law of the Lid is the first law of leadership.

"YOU DON'T KNOW HOW GOOD YOU ARE!"

In my first season coaching at The King's Academy, I had an assistant coach whom I was fortunate to meet earlier that year and get to know. His name is Thadeu Goncalves. Thadeu is a fabulous trainer, originally from Brazil, and at times I would have him run the training sessions so I could observe and make notes. What I remember most vividly, as do the kids, is that Thadeu would always run around the field during the training sessions and in his Brazilian accent be yelling out to the kids, "You don't know how good you are!" He would scream it out to the kids all the time, and basically he was saying, "Keep working, keep training; you don't know how good you are until you work at it, believe, and try."

"You don't know how good you are!"

As coaches, let's try to be careful about assuming how good our players can be. Give them opportunities to flourish. Prepare the proper training environment. Present new challenges for them to fail and succeed so they will have the chance to learn and you will have the chance to teach. Make sure that you are creating those opportunities for them and setting up the right environment. Also make sure that you are not limiting your belief, and thus their belief, on where they can go and what they can accomplish. They will surprise you, and if they do, that probably means you had limitations in your mind on what they could do. If you find yourself utterly surprised, then that shows your accountability—that maybe you were putting limits on them.

THE TWO MOST POWERFUL WORDS IN THE ENGLISH LANGUAGE

When we hear the word "encouragement," I believe most of us think of it as an action word. If you close your eyes and are asked to envision encouragement, you probably see some figure in your life—a parent, relative, coach, or friend—cheering you on or giving you some uplifting words, rallying you, maybe being very animated, and essentially trying to support you and give you confidence and hope. This is a very large part of encouragement and the encouragement most of us prefer to receive. We get fueled by the nice compliments of "good job, keep it up, you're doing well."

Sir Alex Ferguson in *Leading* suggests that the two most powerful words in the English language are "well done."[36]

Someone, almost anyone, putting their arm around us and saying "good job" or "I'm proud of you" is welcomed by the human psyche. Receiving respect and recognition that we've performed well in our responsibilities gives an emotional boost. All of these things are encouraging, and we appreciate the pat on the back and the kind words, and we're more empowered by them.

ENCOURAGEMENT AS ACCOUNTABILITY

Now I'm going to say something here that may take some of you by surprise. It may sound like the antithesis of encouragement, but I want you to be able to recognize that it's not. Accountability is encouraging. "Man, I don't like the sound of that," you think. "That almost sounds like a negative thing. Accountability does not sound like encouragement. That sounds like someone's going to be checking on me, asking me if I got x, y, and z done. I want encouragement so I can feel bolstered and empowered! Accountability makes me feel like I'm being held down and micromanaged." Yuck, right? How many of you feel that way? And this is where I'm going to ask you to take action. Ready?

Wait. Are you really ready? Change the way you look at things, and the way you look at things changes.

When you perceive accountability in a positive light, you receive it as encouraging. The really successful and happiest people in life understand that accountability is encouragement. To be more and do more, really successful people in life seek and crave accountability because they need that encouragement. If as coaches all we do is praise and tell our players "it's okay" all the time and never provide them with instructions or suggestions for their betterment, then there is no chance of substantial improvement.

In an earlier chapter, I discussed having a "standard" as an accountability partner. Holding someone accountable to a standard doesn't mean I have to display an in-their-face, physically or verbally abusive, manipulative attitude. I can be firm and display empathy and compassion when evaluating a person's performance and uphold the standards required of the role. If I never grade my players' performance, then I am not helping them identify areas for improvement. In the moment

---

36. Alex Ferguson and Michael Moritz, *Leading* (New York: Hachette Books, 2015), 118.

that I am evaluating a performance, I am encouraging my players to keep striving for the standard. To be more, do more, have more, and get more out of themselves to reach the standard. If I don't address their performance consistently and don't inform them that they are falling short of the standard, then I am actually discouraging them from getting more. By adding correction and discipline to my encouragement I am setting up my players for the best chance of success. As the leader, if I am allowing them to fall short by not encouraging them through keeping them accountable to their job duties, then I am failing in my duties to help motivate them to grow and achieve more.

And here is the thing: they are craving that from you. The people under your care all want a little encouragement. They all want to be held accountable on some level. Just as I'm explaining to you that you need to change your mindset and realize that being held accountable to a standard, vision, or goal is one of the most powerful forms of encouragement a person can receive, you need to be conveying that same reality to the people around you. That it is a good thing. No! A great thing! It is an honor to have someone in your life willing to hold you accountable to the standards. The accountability you are providing to your players is to continually encourage them to maximize their full potential. Without that accountability to help them measure their progress and let them know where they are and what they still need to do, they will have a hard time fulfilling the promise they made to themselves and you.

SETTING THE STAGE FOR TOUGH CONVERSATIONS

During the season and even in the offseason I check in with my players to update them on where I see them now and to ask them where they see themselves now and into the future. If it's a moment during the season where I feel like they've really fallen short of the standard and I need to address where they are as a player or I need to reprimand them for some failing within our program, I generally start with letting them know these things:

1. We are going to have a tough discussion.
2. This discussion we are having relates to them as a soccer player or within the scope of the team rules and is not a discussion of who they are as a person outside of the game.

3. I remind them of the standard and where I see their performance is in relation to the standard.

I feel that it is necessary to set the stage for the conversation so that the focus can be within the context of our program and not be misconstrued as general statements about character. I believe that clarification is necessary before the conversation begins because many times the statements we make in an evaluation can be taken out of context. I want the context to be clear. When I make a statement about something such as work ethic or focus at practice that is not up to the standard we set, I do not make a general statement about how hard they work or that they are not a hard worker. I relate my comments directly to practice and state that in order to achieve their goal—our goals— they need to be working at the standard we set. If they aren't working at the level of the standard, then we run the risk of not reaching our goal. I remind them of the standard and where I see they are in relation to the standard and the action steps they need to take to reach the standard. They may be working very hard at something else outside of our program. I reserve some compassion and general understanding for life outside the lines. They may have other life things going on that are more important than our sport and the team. If we perceive that to be the case, then I may help them with reevaluating where they are in regards to the team and if they need to be there.

Another tough topic for us as coaches to discuss with our players is the vision of where we see them and where they see themselves. One of our primary roles as coaches is helping players get the most out of themselves while also helping the team. Where we see them positionally may not be where they see themselves. This can be a tough conversation, but it's easier to have with an encouraging heart and when the players know you have their best interest in mind as well as the team's.

When my players tell me where they want to be in the near or far future, I help them evaluate the current situation. "This is where I see you," I say. Or "This is where I think the team needs you," but I almost never tell them that they can't be where they envision themselves. I will generally explain to them what I think it will take to overcome the obstacles in order to achieve their goals, and I help them develop an action plan for doing so.

I continue to check in with them and encourage their pursuit of that goal by keeping them accountable to it.

Now they may decide on their own that they really don't have the want-to or have-to to overcome those obstacles to attain their goals. As a leader, you have to see if you can work with someone who is on your team to discover a new goal that can tap into a have-to and want-to. Sometimes in that discovery process, you'll find that it's time for a player to move on to something that's outside of your direct leadership in another program or organization. I think helping people discover if they fit in your organization and under your leadership is part of your role as the coach. A GET MOR³EE coach is always looking to get the most out of a person's talent and potential. This may be best facilitated in another environment that better fosters their development and offers more opportunity. Helping your players realize this may not benefit your game record, but it will certainly be a win in the coaching people column.

The antonym of "encouragement" is "dissuasion"—the action or process of trying to persuade someone not to take a certain action. Gosh, I don't know how many times in life a person of influence in my life with no ill intent would say these dissuading words: "Well, you know it's really hard, so maybe you should consider something else." "Very few people have the ability to be a college athlete, so that's probably not a reality for you." "Well, you know, not that many people make it, so don't get your hopes up." That has to be one of the dumbest things I've ever heard! How can you make any real pursuit of anything without being hopeful of it being successful?! I'm sure those were the words uttered by Bill Gates or Steve Jobs or Jeff Bezos, right? "Well, I'm going to drop out of school and try to build this software and this computer here, but hey, I'm not real hopeful." Think that was Warren Buffet's pitch to his family and friends when he was raising money to invest? "Hey, let's pool our money, and I'm going to invest it for us, and we plan on getting a return, but don't get your hopes up, just in case we lose everything."

Why would anyone whose job is to coach, lead, teach, or help say something like that to you? Why as leaders would we lead with such dissuading words to someone we are in charge of leading and developing? More than likely it happens when someone has heard the same thing from another person of influence. I heard it too, but I made the decision to reverse it, and you can too.

I said earlier that I believe it's necessary to evaluate where you are. It's okay to say it is going to be hard and also be optimistic that it can be accomplished. I can be completely grounded in the reality of my present situation and still paint a vivid vision of where I want to go. As a coach, I can say "This will be difficult, and very few people have done it" and then follow with helping to evaluate the next steps. I will help strategize where my player wants to go and what needs to be done. I will help my players analyze what resources are needed and whose help they need to accomplish the vision.

A GET MOR³EE coach is an encourager. So, coaches, let's reserve the dissuading talk and be willing to have tough conversations with our players regarding their goals and dreams. I say "tough" because it's tough for us as coaches to resist putting limits on our own mindset based on our experiences. We can base our conversations in reality while also providing practical guidance and still enlarging our players' vision of themselves. It's funny how we work so hard to inspire our people to do so much more but then so quickly pull back on the reins when it's bigger or faster than our own imagination. Leaders, be willing to have the tough conversations. Help your people. And if you can't, just be honest and say "I can't help you with that, because it's outside my purview" and be willing to introduce them to someone who maybe can.

MY COACHES

Encouragement isn't just putting your arm around people and speaking into them. Sometimes encouragement is a kick in the butt. Not literally, but for me it once was literally. In high school, my junior year, I was trying to become a starter on the varsity football team. I played sporadically in a wing-T offense on JV, but I wanted to earn a starting spot at defensive back on varsity. The team was made up of mostly seniors at the time, and I was fighting for a starting position that wasn't mine. Someone else was tapped for the spot. In preseason, we were doing a tackling drill where one defender would go up against two offensive players, one a blocker and the other the ball carrier. We would line up a couple of yards from one another, lying on our backs facing skyward, and when coach would blow the whistle, both sides would jump up, and the defender would have to try to make contact with the first blocker and tackle the ball carrier. I weighed only about 150 pounds at most, so to say that going up against some 200-plus-pound big seniors was a mismatch is no understatement. This literally was like a scene from the movie *Rudy*. The coaches generally try to line you up with people of similar size, but the drill gets going and guys are jumping in and out, and if you want to get in sometimes you just have to jump in.

Two big seniors drop down on offense, and I want to get in so I jump down on defense. Coach blows the whistle. I flip over real quick, go to make contact—and get pancaked. Just absolutely blown out. Like Wile E. Coyote getting peeled off the pavement run over. Now usually you flip out of the drill and others flip in, but Coach yells, "Do it again." We drop down. He blows the whistle, and I get semi-truck all-eighteen-wheels run over again. At this point, Coach goes somewhat ballistic on me. Does the old classic football scene where he grabs me by my facemask so he can look me square in my eyes and gives me some good "tough love" verbal encouragement. I could not even tell you what he was saying, but I think he was unhappy with my performance. He barks out to get back down there and do it **again**.

At this point I'm embarrassed. I've got tears, sweat, or Coach's spittle stinging my eyes. I'm lying on my back looking up into the sun when Coach's shadow leans back over me again. Still fired up, he sternly directs some words of instruction to me, and again I have no idea what he said, but then—and I remember this clearly—after his shadow lifted back up and the sun reappeared, this kick. I feel this kick right in my kinda lower rib buttock side, with the words like "C'mon on, Slay, what are you, some kinda momma's boy?!" Now this is all happening so fast. Probably less than 15 seconds after me getting bulldozed for the second time, Coach in my face, me back on the ground, the encouragement kick, and now me in complete tears and pissed off mad. Angry? Mad? Either way, I'm just flush with fury, and then the whistle. I fired out of there like the fastest 150-pound tank on earth I could be.

Now I can't say I pancaked the other guy. He still had at least 50 pounds on me, but something good happened, and we all ended up in a pile with me having performed some type of tackle on the ball carrier. They yanked us out, and I went to the back of the circle, still angry with tears, sweat, or spittle in my eyes. I got some slaps on the helmet and some "good jobs" and that was it.

A couple years later, after I graduated, we were at Coach's house and talking about different stories, and I asked him if he remembered the time he "kicked me." He did not. I recalled to him the story of him calling me a momma's boy, and he laughed hysterically.

Now I'm not telling you as coaches to go around kicking players. Coach V had known me most of my life, and there was a relationship there. I exaggerate it as a true kick. It was more like a quick nudge. One of those slaps-on-the-butt types of encouragement you get with the "Let's go!" when you take the field. I just happened to be lying on my backside on the ground. The whole experience was the true "kick" of encouragement that I needed at the time. In reflection, I now understand that he saw more in me than what I was giving and could not let that moment when I was failing slip away. He could have just pulled me out and moved on or thrown some guys down that were my size, but I chose to jump in there with the big guys, so he made me own it. He held me accountable to my actions and had to keep me in there so that he could see and I could see if I had it in me. Coach V needed to see if he could get more out of me, and he also needed to see if I could recognize that I had more in me. I started every game that year on a 9–1 team.

About midway through the season, I'm playing cornerback in a game against Belle Glade Christian. Their team had a very good quarterback and a really good running back and this like 6-foot, 4-inch, 300-pound offensive lineman they kept running behind. I think it was like early fourth quarter in a very tight game, and we were lined up on defense. Their offense was driving and has just crossed the fifty-yard line. Their quarterback snaps the ball and starts rolling out to my side. They've got receivers running routes into my area, and I feel all of our team, including the linebackers, flowing into my zone in the flats. Somehow I recognize that their running back has come out on this route into the space our linebackers just vacated to my left. I know the quarterback is looking for him, so before he's even released the ball, I leave my zone and just break towards the running back, and sure enough here comes the ball, and I get my first interception.

I start trying to run up the field and see the big 6-foot, 4-inch, 300-pound lineman in my path, so I make this big end-around run to avoid him and head straight to the sideline. I was told later my eyes became as big as saucers when I saw that giant kid in front of me. I turn up the sideline–I can feel the chase now—and I see one of my teammates running down the sideline in front of me, blocking **no one**. I remember thinking to myself, *What is he doing, like block one of these dudes chasing me?!* And then I see the good running back kid out of the corner of my eye, barreling down on me, so I step out of bounds real quick into our sideline, and a few people catch me.

It's a hectic scene after a turnover. Someone takes the ball out of my hands as our offense runs out onto the field, and probably a few people are around congratulating me. I think our offense goes down the field real quick and scores, and that kinda puts the game away, so my interception was a big momentum changer.

I'm standing on the sideline, and I feel a big arm come around me, embrace me, and pull me in, and I look up and it's Coach V. He's smiling and says something like "Wow, you got lucky being so far out of position," and I try to explain that I saw it, and he just gives me another squeeze, laughs, looks at me and is like "Good job; now go get in at quarterback the next series."

Another example of accountability I remember is from when I was a twelve-year-old kid playing little league baseball. I had been on the same team, the Lions, with the same coach for four years. Coach Clanton was my coach that whole time, and he was the father of one of the teammates I started out with. At age twelve, I was one of the oldest kids on the team, as it was a nine-to-twelve-year-old age group. Coach was asking me to pitch that year, and I had never been a pitcher, and to be honest I was being a bit of a baby about it. He asked me to do it, and I pouted, mostly out of fear, I believe, of being on that stage. As a catcher, I was always hiding behind a mask and tons of gear. Was kinda protected, and I liked it. People knew I was the catcher for that team, but I liked that seeming anonymity, I think. Our team needed some older arms, so it made sense for me to try it at least, but I was dismissive and frankly pouted.

I remember one day in practice Coach asked me to pitch again, and I had some kind of little tantrum about it, and when my mom pulled up to practice, I went and jumped in the car and I guess maybe said something like I was quitting. Well, Coach Clanton did not let me get away with that.

In a few seconds, he was at my mom's car window, and he let me have it. Can't recall the exact words, but he basically called me out for pouting, quitting, not being a team player. And he did it respectfully. There was no cursing or abusive language. Give credit to my mom for letting him let me have it. Not sure if I went back out to practice that day, but I think it was still in my mind to quit. Baseball usually got boring for me anyways, and I didn't like being pulled out of my comfort zone either. My parents explained to me though that once we started something, we needed to finish it. If I didn't want to play again after the season, then that was fine, but I had to finish.

I went back the next day and apologized to Coach, and it was a huge life lesson for me. I spent four great years with Coach Clanton as my little league baseball coach, from 9 to 12 years old. Those were some very formative years in my life and I expect for most kids that age. He was teaching and coaching, and I can recall some skill things we did, but the thing I remember most clearly in it all was the day he called me out when I said I wanted to quit. Coach Clanton holding me accountable, not quitting on me, and he and my parents not allowing me to quit on my team was the biggest lesson of all.

A couple of years later, I was playing varsity soccer for my high school as a freshman. We didn't have a JV, and a few weeks into the season, I still wasn't starting. This is a great example of how easy it can be for a kid to quickly forget a lesson or not recognize it at the time. I tried to quit my little league baseball team two years earlier because I was frustrated, and here I was, ready to quit again. I recall walking into the athletic director's office when my coach was in there after a game and telling them I wanted to quit because I wasn't playing.

Now, we had like seven or eight freshmen starting on this team already, and we hadn't won a game, and I was a five-foot-nothing goalkeeper who had barely played in middle school. It would have been very easy to toss aside one more freshman and say "Okay, if that's how you feel, then so be it." The AD (athletic director), Rick Dixon, talked to me and encouraged me to stick with it, and so I did. Within a couple more weeks, I was starting and getting more playing time, and then I played almost every game in goal for our team for the remainder of my high school career. I went on to play college soccer at Palm Beach Atlantic College, where I met my wife and many of my friends. I coach at a high school now that I love and that provides a great education for my children. It's been a joy to coach those kids the past three seasons, making it to the district finals every year and winning the championship this past season and being voted Coach of the Year. If the coach and AD had let that bratty fourteen-year-old kid quit playing soccer, what might I have missed out on? I'm eternally grateful for their investment in me.

Recognize the power of encouragement and the power of encouragement through accountability.

SCOUTING REPORT LESSONS
- ▶ Encouragement is powerful and necessary for an organization to flourish and grow.
- ▶ Accountability is also encouragement, and we need to understand the power of encouragement through accountability.
- ▶ Encouragement needs to be routine, meaning it is consistent and intentional.
- ▶ The Law of Belief as Encouragement states that the players' level of belief in themselves is capped by the level of belief the coach expresses in his or her team.
- ▶ Remember to set the stage for tough conversations with your players.
- ▶ Coaching is the exponential multiplier of talent and potential.
- ▶ Talent doesn't always win!
- ▶ Encouragement is the fuel that leads to empowerment.

GET MOR³EE: REMEMBER YOUR MOTIVES. OWN THE STRUGGLES. KEEP YOUR EYE ON THE PRIZE. ALLOW ACCOUNTABILITY TO FUEL YOU, NOT LIMIT YOU. LET IT ALL EMPOWER YOU.

COACHES' BOX: AN ENCOURAGEMENT PRACTICE
The honest truth is that not all of us are great natural encouragers. Even if we are, there are days when we are feeling discouraged ourselves, so how are we supposed to encourage others? This is an exercise I use to help me with my encouragement practices with my players.

Take out a sheet of paper and something to write with, or just use the notes app on your phone. Set a timer and give yourself a minimum of five minutes to complete the exercise, but if it takes ten to fifteen minutes, that's okay. You will feel good about it when you are done and more equipped to provide encouragement.

Now think about each of your players and write out what you value about them. Don't make a list, but write out a few sentences or maybe a few paragraphs about what you value in each of them. What do they bring to the team as individuals that you find valuable? What about their interactions with you or the team do you appreciate? Is there something in each player's character you find yourself or other players admiring? Is there something in their practice or game performances that is special? What unique talents does each individual bring to the team? After you write out the sentences, then read them over and circle, highlight, or underline a few of the words that you feel best describe each player.

Now that you are equipped with your players' traits that you value, make it a priority this week to share with each player what you value about him or her as an individual. Do it off to the side or in a thirty-second one-on-one pause with the player before or after practice or a game. I prefer after practice to reinforce the practice qualities just demonstrated or before a game to build confidence and belief.

The next part is to seek an opportunity to praise the player to other people with the individual present. Maybe it's in a team meeting or in front of the player's parents. Find a moment in the presence of school officials, teachers, or opponents, even. If you can't find a moment, create one. Find an opportunity to extol each individual's best traits to those people.

> Make it a point to do this exercise with all of your players. If you are not a natural encourager, this practice will help you perform your role as chief encouragement officer and lead your players to empowerment.
> **Encourage often. Praise in public. Criticize in private.**

A VEHICLE ANALOGY OF GET MOR³EE

In this chapter, we've been discussing encouragement and how powerful and necessary it is for an organization to grow and be fueled. It seems simple, but I expect that some readers are still trying to wrap their mind around and fully comprehend the necessity of encouragement in the formula. I'm going to paint a picture and use the image of a vehicle as another description of the encouragement property in the GET MOR³EE formula. Hop on board!

Okay, imagine some type of vehicle. A car, truck, jet, Humvee, or whatever vehicle you would like to imagine. As we do this exercise you may want to alter or change your vehicle, and that's okay. Do it. You are the coach, and you have the power to change the vehicle to get you where you want to go.

Now as we said at the beginning of the book, we start with **motivation**. Imagine motivation as starting with where you want to go. I've plotted a location on a map or entered some coordinates into my GPS. Working backwards from my desired destination to where I'm starting from in my current location, I've analyzed the route, the terrain, the possible obstacles, elements I may encounter, and so on. We need to build the vehicle with these things in mind. Where do I want to go? Where do I have to go to get there? If I'm going to the end of the street, maybe my vehicle is a bicycle or skateboard. If I'm going to Mars, then I need to create a different vehicle for the longer, more arduous journey. It comes back to "begin with the end in mind." So, I have the motivation for where we are going. I have the plans for my vehicle. Let's start building.

Let's imagine **ownership** as the major components of the frame, supports, and so on. Ownership is the foundation of our car, upon which everything else is attached and built. It's also the part of the vehicle that is taking the pounding and the pressure when you're on the bumpy road and getting wrecked. The frame needs to be built to withstand the journey you think you'll be taking. Truck frames and car frames are different, right? And a truck frame built for cruising around town is different than a truck frame built for towing. If we assume ownership of this vehicle, we are responsible for building the foundation of the vehicle and everything that attaches onto it. The people on your team join in that ownership and help you. They are the additional screws and bolts that help strengthen the foundation when they also take ownership in the integrity of the vehicle.

Responsibility would be, say, your steering wheel, mirrors, headlights, taillights, brakes, gas pedal, and many of the control and safety features, like the airbags and seatbelts. You need to adjust your mirrors and make sure the lights, blinkers, horn, brakes, and seatbelts all work. You are responsible for your vehicle and the people traveling with you in it. When I learned to drive a school bus, before I started driving the instructor took a week to go through the checklist of what I was responsible for once I stepped behind the wheel. As a player or coach, I have to be responsible for my vehicle. Maybe I'm navigating or checking the oil or taking my turn driving the team's vehicle, but I'm always responsible for taking the wheel of my own vehicle. No one else can drive my vehicle. Teammates can give me a push, help me make repairs, or give me some gas, but I have to drive. As leaders, we are responsible for the team vehicle. We also need to convey to the individual players on our team that they are at the wheel of their own vehicle. They are the driver. They are responsible for their contribution and journey.

Respect is the engine, as I imagine it. It's the building block of a person's power and drive. Respect is a recognition or admiration or belief of what someone can or has accomplished. The engine is the respect factor. The greater the level of respect I have for myself, my team, and the process, the more potential power and drive in my engine.

Rewards are all the nice shiny stuff like the chrome alloy wheels and the leather seats. Or heat and air conditioning in the seats! Rewards are the fancy trim, sunroof, and moonroof. It's the high-end features—surround sound, lane assist, self-driving, DVD player, Wi-Fi capability. It looks good on you. It feels good on you. You have a feeling of accomplishment with the finishing of this car.

So now you have this whole car put together. You know where you want to go. The vehicle has a nice body, a strong frame, and an engine equal to the task. The inside looks good and feels good and makes you feel equipped to take this journey, but this vehicle still can't go anywhere without the fuel.

Encouragement is the fuel, so that when you put your foot down on the pedal you put that encouragement into the engine, and that's what makes the vehicle run. With a vehicle, the more fuel fed to the engine and the better the quality of the fuel, the faster the vehicle can move and the better the performance. Encouragement is the fuel for your players and team. The more encouragement you give and the higher the quality of encouragement, the faster your team can run and the better the performance. You can get up running fast and put on the cruise control in some situations, and as long as no obstacles get in your way, you can cruise until either you reach your destination or you run out of gas.

We know it never happens that way though, right? You have to be able to make minor to major adjustments, depending on what obstacles you come up against, the car you're driving, and the journey you are on. You have to stop and top off your fuel tank every once in a while, as every good leader knows. You get stalled and or hit a slow or bumpy patch of road, and you might be tempted just to rev back up and keep going. Have you ever been stuck in the mud with your car or seen someone else's vehicle stuck in the mud? Many times, the first instinct is just to try to power through to free the vehicle, and sometimes that works. Most of the time the driver just ends up spinning the wheels and burying the vehicle deeper in the mud. In the process, everyone and everything just gets covered with mud and exhausts their energy.

What do wise leaders do? Wise leaders use these roadblocks and setbacks as opportunities to top off the encouragement tank. They use these moments to fill back up. Get the map out, check the GPS, make sure they are on the right road or plot a course to get back on the right road, or maybe they have to take an alternate route, but they always try to fuel back up for the next part of the journey. If you get going good again and have that open stretch of road where you are flying, you definitely don't want to have to stop because you are low on gas and failed to fuel up when you had the opportunity. Encouragement is the fuel that makes everything run. ***Encouragement is the fuel that leads to empowerment.***

CHAPTER TEN
EMPOWERMENT

The empowerment property in the GET MOR³EE formula is a person's self-confidence to take initiative to do more, which fuels their creativity, imagination, and passion and creates even greater momentum and motivation.

> *"Leadership is not defined by the exercise of power but by the capacity to increase the sense of power among those led. The most essential work of the leader is to create more leaders."* (Mary Parker Follett)[37]

The most essential work of the coach is to empower more players. GET MOR³EE is my formula for unlocking that capacity within me. How can I empower this person? How can I lead my players from motivation to empowerment?

TOP-DOWN MANAGEMENT

Many coaches prefer the top-down management style, which can be effective, but I find it to be an unempowering process. It can become an exhausting process for the coach and players. Coaches give directives, and players respond to directives and execute directives and then wait for the next directive. The top-down management style conditions people to stay in line, wait, and respond to instructions.

GET MOR³EE coaching empowers players in every level of your program to think—for a change—and to seek solutions or new opportunities on their own without constant input from the coach. It shakes off the chains, allowing players to assume greater responsibility

---

37. Mary Parker Follett, *Creative Experience* (New York: Longmans, Green and Co., 1930).

for their contribution to the team. It eliminates the need for constant oversight from the coaching staff and encourages the players to become invested in holding each other accountable.

This statement from the chapters on **motivation** and **respect** is worth recalling because it all leads to **empowerment**:

Power comes from the vision, not the volume.

An empowering vision calls out so much louder than you can ever speak. The true show of someone's leadership and authority is the ability to grant power to another person. When you are really able to instill into people the integrity of your position, leadership, and authority is when you are able to give power and empower the other people around you. They will give more and risk more than you can ever ask of them because they are empowered by the rewards of the vision. They will let you lead them. They will follow you, because you gave them the power to see and believe in the vision you set before them.

COACHES' BOX: EMPOWERMENT FOR DIFFERENT AGE GROUPS

I believe empowerment is contextual to the age group you are coaching. Younger kids like U8 (under 8) should be empowered to have fun. Nine-to-twelve-year-old kids still generally need to be told what to do and what you want from them, but start inviting them into the discussion. Even if they don't quite understand yet, it challenges them to start thinking about the game in different ways. It stimulates learning. You may not call it empowerment, but the thirteen and up age group, the high school kids, can soar in an empowering environment. Grant them permission to try. Try what, you ask? Try anything you say. Open up the conversation and encourage their input. Allow them to dream big, and help them to dream bigger. Let them lead. It can be difficult for both coaches and players to release themselves from the top-down management style. The need for controls or perceived need can be hard to let go of. If you can find a way to release yourself of the outcome, it's easy to give power.

THE HILL

Halfway through our 2018–19 championship season, our record did not look good. We were roughly a month into the season and had one victory in the win column. That is when we took to the hill. I decided I needed to find the highest hill in our area. Instead of training as usual, we loaded up onto a bus and drove to "the hill." Now in reality there aren't many large hills in South Florida. We just happen to have an old landfill that the county turned into a park nearby that would work just fine. In college, I ran these same hills.

Brian McMahon, the current head men's soccer coach at my alma mater, Palm Beach Atlantic University, had shared his offseason fitness program with me. Now, Brian has been a very successful coach at the college level. He won a NAIA national title with Belhaven University and has been named Coach of the Year for a handful of prestigious associations. At Palm Beach Atlantic University, his teams have won multiple conference titles, been ranked as high as #2 in the country, and advanced as far as the Elite 8 in the NCAA D2 National Tournament. Inside his summer fitness program, Coach Mac, as he is called, interlays stories and quotes from NFL legends Jerry Rice and Roger Craig and other players who used to run these hills with Rice during his playing days with the San Francisco 49ers. He speaks of "the hill" often in the manual, extolling the virtues of finding "your hill" so it can push you beyond your expectations of what you are capable of. That's where the idea of the hill came from.

So I load the boys up on the bus, and we drive to the landfill park to an actual hill. With younger players, sometimes the visual is much more effective. I walk them out to the base of the hill for the full effect. It is a double hill with about a 45-degree grade, and the first section is about 15 to 20 yards up the embankment, and then it flattens out for a few yards, and then up another 40 to 50 yards, depending upon what section you are on at the crest. The hill is completely covered in grass in most areas, with barren dirt areas in some sections. My idea was that we would start on the shorter end, and as the boys came back down the hill we would move down a few yards, and each ascent would be a little bit higher and harder. The directive was to sprint straight up the hill as fast as they could.

I line the boys up and send them up the hill, and they take off with enthusiasm. At the top of the first hill where it flattens out, a few boys fall, unaware that it is flat, but jump up and keep going. After they descend back down the hill, I read a quote to them about the hill from Coach Mac's summer training program to motivate them for the next climb.

> *"The late Walter Payton, Hall of Fame running back for the Chicago Bears, had told Craig (Roger Craig) that the key to thriving in their position was endurance training, and that the key to endurance was taking on the steepest hill he could find."*

"Go!" I shout, and up again they go and then back down. I read to them another quote about the hill.

> *"'It was the toughest thing I ever did in my life,' Craig said. 'I threw up a couple of times going up this trail. I was a football player. I'd never run that far; I was only good for 100 yards. I ran track and stuff, but as far as running four miles, that was unheard of.' Ting (coach) said, 'Just hang in there.' So, I did it for a few weeks with him. And I started loving it. I could feel it. I was getting in great shape. So, I introduced it to some of my teammates. I said, 'Man, you guys have to come out here and run this trail.'"*

Again, the boys ascend and descend, now gasping for air. I read them another quote.

> *"The Hill soon went from training ground to proving ground, an initiation to show what it took to become a champion. Are you tough enough? Are you dedicated enough? How much are you willing to suffer? Craig said they eventually had a group of up to 25 players running the Hill. To this day, the tradition endures. On May 7, 2012, not long after the 49ers drafted receiver AJ Jenkins, Rice tweeted him, 'I'm getting in top shape to get you up that hill.' Jenkins never took Rice up on his offer; he had 0 catches as a rookie."*

We repeat this a few more times, and at the base we are making our way toward the higher sections of the hill. We are about halfway to our destination of the highest point of the hill. When the boys go up this time, a couple of them hit a hole at the top of the first section and completely wipe out. I climb to where the hole is, and it is big. What makes it worse is that you can't even see it because so much grass is covering it. So before they come back down, I stand in front of the hole so they know where it is and yell up to them to not run down this way.

As they descend and the players run by, there's one boy directly behind me who I don't see. I move to the side to start to climb down and walk around the hole, and he goes right into the hole behind me and turns his ankle. Within seconds, it swells up like a softball. I help him down the hill, and at this point I'm just worried about this player's ankle and thinking how I may need to get him right to the trainer and I hope it's not broken. My next thought is that our hill running for today is over. I leave the boys there with him and run the 300 yards back to the bus to get some ice. I'm gone for a good ten minutes as I dig around trying to find a plastic bag, then scoop some ice, and then finally start to make my way back.

As I start to head back to them, I notice the players running up the hill! I'm not sure how many times they've gone up, but by the time I make it back over to our injured player and put the ice on his ankle and prop it up, the rest of the team is far enough down from us that it looks like they've run the hill four or five more times. As I sit with the player for a minute, evaluating his ankle, I can hear the rest of the team as they get down to the bottom of the hill. They don't have my paper with the quotes, but one of them has replaced me, giving a motivational quote before running back up the hill!

They go up again, and when they come down another player steps up to give the motivational quote, and away they go again. I decide to make my way down towards them, but at this point I don't want to interrupt so I just listen as yet another player steps up and gives an inspirational quote. I climb to the top of the hill where they will be making their final run, and they take off again to meet me there to conclude our hill running for the day.

At the top of the hill, I invite them to look out at all they could see that wasn't visible down in the valley. I ask them if things look different from this elevated perspective. From their new vantage point, could they value all the hard work they had just put in? Where could it take them?

What those boys did for the second half of that run was an example of feeling empowered. As I left to tend to our injured player, they could have just sat there and waited. Instead, they picked up and continued on and got the job done. Many times, as a youth in sports, I never felt empowered to be, do, or say anything other than what the coach told me, for fear of being reprimanded. I recall times when I saw or anticipated things I could or should have done. If not given the time to think about it, my instincts usually led me the right way, but if given the time to think about it, I would be afraid to try something new or act on those instincts for fear of failure and a coach's wrath. Those boys could have sat there in fear that I might get on them for continuing on. A top-down coach probably would. I was proud of them for taking the initiative because at the end of the day, it's their hill to climb.

The hill became a thing for us, and we went back several times, although on a paved and more predictable running area, and continued to go climb the hill. One of the quotes I read about the hill was about doing what others would not do and that I believed that none of our competition would be climbing hills.

In the early part of the season, we had lost a lot of close games in the last few minutes, and to change that outcome we had to do something that no one else was willing to do. In the game after our first hill climb, we scored 11 goals in our second victory of the season. After our last hill climb, we proceeded to go on an 8–4 run, shutting out six teams in our eight victories. Three of those shutouts were in the playoffs. We went on to win the district championship for only the third time in school history and advanced through to the regional quarterfinals for only the second time in school history.

A POEM: THE BRILLIANCE OF COMMITMENT

A poem by William Hutchinson Murray has become a staple of our team. I share it with my players every season, and I share it with you here. It's been a powerful aide to me in stepping out of my comfort zone to share the GET MOR³EE formula with you.

"Until one is committed, there is hesitancy, the chance to draw back, always ineffectiveness. Concerning all acts of initiative (and creation), there is one elementary truth, the ignorance of which kills countless ideas and splendid plans: that the moment one definitely commits oneself, then Providence moves too. All sorts of things occur to help one that would never otherwise have occurred. A whole stream of events issues from the decision, raising in one's favour all manner of unforeseen incidents and meetings and material assistance which no man could have dreamt would have come his way. I have learned a deep respect for one of Goethe's couplets:

'Whatever you can do, or dream you can, begin it.

Boldness has genius, power, and magic in it!'"

(Attributed to William Hutchinson Murray)

I'M IN THE PEOPLE BUSINESS

Almost two decades ago, I read the book *What Color Is Your Parachute?*[38] In the book, the reader is asked a series of questions to which the reader is asked to answer with a response of people, information, or things. I discovered that when faced with the decision of choosing people, information, or things, people made up five of my answers, information made up one, and zero of my answers contained things! This opened my eyes to the fact that people are very important to me and I don't care much about things. I think the attraction to people is the coach in me. I love to see people succeed. I enjoy helping people tap into their potential and cultivate their talents. How that connects to my strengths and passion is that I want and need to use them when working with people to be most effective.

For the past decade I've owned a real estate company, and we deal with buildings and properties and land, but our business is really a reflection of what people need and want. The buildings and homes and what's done with them are all reflections of what the community is doing and what the people who live there need and want.

I am a coach. I coach people. I'm coaching a game, and there is a ball and a field with boundaries and rules and goals, but it's ultimately all about the people playing the game. I'm coaching the people within the game. If I know how to coach people and get the most out of them and empower them to achieve more, then I can lead in almost any industry. I don't necessarily need to be highly skilled or knowledgeable at the day-

---

38. Richard N. Bolles, *What Color is Your Parachute?* (Berkeley: Ten Speed Press, 2004).

to-day functions of the job or sport or whatever it is I am leading people in. It certainly helps to have a general understanding, but as a leader if I'm empowering the people in those roles who are more skilled than I am at those functions, then I just need to encourage and inspire them. I need to provide them with tools and support and give them permission to be amazing at what they do, and they will take care of much of the rest. My priority should be to take care of my people and create the environment for them to prosper and succeed in. When as coaches we empower individuals inside our team and align the individual with team goals, the team will have the ability to accomplish so much more than the individual can alone, and we will exceed most people's expectations.

In the GET MOR^{3}EE formula the product of reaching empowerment is increased momentum. Read on to find out how this newly created momentum benefits your team to reach even greater heights of success and achievement.

> *The most powerful two words in the English language are "Well done!"*
>
> *The most important three words in the English language are "I love you."*
>
> *The most empowering four words in the English language are "I believe in you."*

SCOUTING REPORT LESSONS

- ▶ Empowerment is a person's self-confidence to take initiative in doing more, which fuels their creativity, imagination, and passion and creates even greater momentum and motivation.
- ▶ The most essential work of the coach is to empower more players.
- ▶ **Power comes from the vision, not the volume.**
- ▶ The product of reaching empowerment in the GET MOR^{3}EE formula is increased momentum.

GET MOR^{3}EE: REMEMBER YOUR MOTIVES. OWN THE STRUGGLES. KEEP YOUR EYE ON THE PRIZE. ALLOW ACCOUNTABILITY TO FUEL YOU, NOT LIMIT YOU. LET IT ALL EMPOWER YOU.

CHAPTER ELEVEN
MOMENTUM

The benefit of empowering players through the GET MOR³EE formula is increased momentum. Leadership guru John Maxwell calls this The Law of the Big Mo. He states that "momentum is a leader's best friend." Maxwell says this is "because many times [momentum] is the only thing that makes the difference between losing and winning. When you have no momentum, even the simplest tasks seem impossible ... On the other hand, when you have momentum on your side, the future looks bright, obstacles appear small, and troubles seem inconsequential."[39]

I'll borrow an example from Jim Collins in *Good to Great* to help describe the power of momentum. Collins's description of a flywheel is a great illustration of the GET MOR³EE formula cycle of motivation to empowerment.

> Picture a huge, heavy flywheel—a massive metal disk mounted horizontally on an axle, about 30 feet in diameter, 2 feet thick, and weighing about 5,000 pounds. Now imagine that your task is to get the flywheel rotating on the axle as fast and long as possible. Pushing with great effort, you get the flywheel to inch forward, moving almost imperceptibly at first. You keep pushing and, after two or three hours of persistent effort, you get the flywheel to complete one entire turn. You keep pushing, and the flywheel begins to move a bit faster, and with continued great effort, you move it around a second rotation. You keep pushing in a consistent direction. Three turns ... four ... five ... six ... the flywheel builds up speed ... seven ... eight ... you keep pushing ... nine ... ten ... it

---

39. John C. Maxwell, *The 21 Irrefutable Laws of Leadership* (Nashville: Thomas Nelson, 1998 and 2007), 197

builds momentum ... eleven ... twelve ... moving faster with each turn ... twenty ... thirty ... fifty ... a hundred.

Then, at some point—breakthrough! The momentum of the thing kicks in in your favor, hurling the flywheel forward, turn after turn ... whoosh! ... its own heavy weight working for you. You're pushing no harder than during the first rotation, but the flywheel goes faster and faster. Each turn of the flywheel builds upon work done earlier, compounding your investment of effort. A thousand times faster, then ten thousand, then a hundred thousand. The huge heavy disk flies forward, with almost unstoppable momentum.

Now suppose someone came along and asked, "What was the one big push that caused this thing to go so fast?" You wouldn't be able to answer; it's just a nonsensical question. Was it the first push? The second? The fifth? The hundredth? No! It was *all* of them added together in an overall accumulation of effort applied in a consistent direction. Some pushes may have been bigger than others, but any single heave—no matter how large—reflects a small fraction of the entire cumulative effect upon the flywheel.[40]

At first it takes a lot of effort to begin to move the flywheel forward, but as you are able to get the flywheel through each rotation it gets easier to turn as you build momentum. If you're a person who enjoys cross-training, imagine a large truck tire and the effort, force, and strength needed to try to roll it and get it moving and keep it balanced. Once you get that truck tire rolling, don't be standing in its way!

As coaches, we are continually striving to build momentum with our players and teams. Once you are able to get through maybe one rotation of motivation to empowerment in the GET MOR³EE formula, you've developed some momentum. Each time you reach empowerment, you want to continue the process. As you reassess the individual, check the motivation. Do your players feel like they have some ownership and understand what it means to be a stakeholder in the process? Are they managing their responsibilities and taking responsibility for their actions? Do they feel respected, and do they show respect for others around them and the organization? Are the rewards (tangible and intangible) still in

40. Jim Collins, *Good To Great* (New York: Harper Business, 2001).

line and still strong enough to keep them motivated? Encouragement is one of the most important factors as this wheel gets turning and spinning. As leaders, we need to constantly be providing encouragement, which is like nourishment for this process. Encouragement is the fuel that leads to empowerment.

HOW MOMENTUM CREATED A CHAMPIONSHIP TEAM

By this point, you've read about the boys' high school soccer team that I coach and our exploits from this past season. You know we struggled at the start of our season, only winning two of our first ten games. You know we overcame our struggles in the second half of the season to become the district champions. What I did not share with you was how **momentum** propelled us into the last few games of the season and allowed us to dominate the district playoffs.

We lost one game in the two weeks leading up to the district playoffs, and it was a 2–1 loss to the team that beat us 7–1 in our first preseason game. We were missing three starters that night, and two of them were senior captains. In the four games leading up to the start of districts, including that one loss, we won three of the four games, recording two shutouts and outscoring opponents 17 to 2. We rolled into the district playoffs knowing that in the regular season, we had not defeated any of the teams we were possibly to play. The first game, the district quarterfinal, we won handily 4–1 against a team we tied 3–3 in the regular season. The goal they did score was awarded on a penalty kick with a minute or so left in the game. For the district semifinal, we were facing one of our rivals and the number one seeded team in the district. They defeated us 3–2 in the regular season. By the end of the first half we had jumped out to a 4–0 lead. We came over to the sideline for halftime, and it was the most relaxed and confident I had seen our team all season. Barely a word was spoken as we sat there waiting for the second half to start, because there was nothing more to say. We finished the game with a 6–0 victory. We advanced to the district finals for the third year in a row to face the same team that had defeated us the previous two years and was the reigning state champion. Just three weeks earlier we fell to them 2–0 in the regular season. Now we rode the momentum of the previous six games to a 1–0 victory in winning the district championship. In our first 7 games of the season, our record was 1 win and 6 losses, and we had scored 10 goals to our opponents 22, with zero shutouts. In our last 7 games leading up to and including the district championship, our record was 6 wins and 1 loss, and we scored 27 goals while only allowing our opponents to find the net 4 times during that stretch and recording 4 shutouts.

That district championship victory was built on the back of three years' worth of momentum. We were building the final half of our season during the first half of our season, with the GET MOR³EE formula. We used the same formula as the previous two seasons and moved from motivation to empowerment and then rode the momentum into the finals. We used the same formula in the offseason to build the momentum heading into our season. The momentum of the district championship created three first team All-County player selections, two second team honors, one United Soccer Coaches All-State Team selection, one Palm Beach County Player of the Year Award, and one Sun-Sentinel Coach of the Year Award. The momentum continues, as my boys are now recruiting their friends and organizing workouts in the offseason. The product of reaching empowerment in the GET MOR³EE formula is increased momentum.

Success breeds interest.

People are naturally drawn to success. When we see it, we become curious, and we want to know why and how people or teams are successful. Billions of dollars and thousands of hours each year are committed to explore, study, train for, and pursue success and excellence. It is why you are reading this book. You want to be more successful in your coaching career and experience more success with the individuals on your team.

The buildup of momentum in the GET MOR³EE formula creates that success. As you cycle through each rotation of the formula, you may find yourself experiencing a little more success. Success breeds interest.

As you put the GET MOR³EE formula into practice, you may find that new athletes and more talented players are attracted to your program. More opportunities present themselves for your players. More material assistance may come your way. Other training opportunities and access to different technologies become available. People start appearing from seemingly nowhere to offer assistance, because success breeds interest. Increased momentum brings you greater success in your coaching career and with your teams and players.

THE GET MOR³EE MERRY-GO-ROUND

When I think about the image of the GET MOR³EE cycle with youth I always picture an old merry-go-round in a park. Not every park had one, but if there was one, kids were surely drawn to it. The more people present in the park, the greater activity there was around the merry-go-round.

Now take a few seconds and imagine yourself in a park. You are standing in front of the merry-go-round. You feel the sun glinting through the trees as the branches sway in the breeze. There are birds chirping and dogs barking in the distance. You hear the sound of play as children and families commune in the park. One adventurous child goes over and recruits some other children to get the merry-go-round spinning. Seemingly out of nowhere, more and more kids appear and jump on to join the ride. Kids and parents are running to get the merry-go-round turning. You are one of them.

As it starts spinning, you can't keep running with it. It's going too fast. You've created momentum now, so you stop and watch as it spins around, enjoying the show and the laughter and the good results. Now, if no one continues to push the merry-go-round, the momentum will eventually fade, slow down, and stop. It is possible to get it going again, but a lot of effort is required—after restarting it a few times you would be exhausted. "Can't do it anymore," you say to the kids. "I'm done."

The other option as the merry-go-round gets going is, instead of just stepping back and watching, give a little push every time it comes around. A little encouragement keeps it going. You can continue to give it little pushes and keep it spinning with less effort than starting over. Sometimes, you give a few quick pushes; other times, you see it's moving well, so you can let it spin. Each push of the merry-go-round is tantamount to giving encouragement to a player or your team.

Many times, as leaders, coaches, teachers, and managers, we can be very good at getting the wheel spinning. We tend to put a lot of effort into the ramp-up. We have a big vision that excites us, so in the beginning it is easy to begin to encourage the people around us to come together to produce and perform. As we gain momentum and things get moving, we allow other things to take priority. We see our people doing well, or we think they are doing well, and we take a step back, and the wheel begins to slow. We look away, and it's so gradual sometimes that we don't even notice until we look back and it's almost stopped. Remember, *"Encouragement is the fuel that leads to empowerment."*

The most important thing we can do as leaders as the wheel is spinning and the people are running is to continually fuel it with encouragement. Give it a little push. Once the elements of ownership, responsibility, respect, and rewards are in place, use encouragement to achieve momentum. Encourage the players when they fail and fall; encourage them to continue to strive for their goals the closer they get. Applaud them when they do, and then help them renew those goals and motivation as they experience success.

As the merry-go-round begins to slow, some kids start to hang off the side and kick off the ground to keep it moving. One kid might even jump off and help you push the merry-go-round and then jump back on. Other kids will see this and think, "Hey, I want to be a part of that," without you even asking them to help. These are self-motivated people who feel empowered.

Now some of the kids may be hesitant. They aren't sure if it's okay for them to push or run alongside you. They look to you for permission and affirmation. What will you say to them? Are you observing their motivation to join and help and be a part of your organization? Do you recognize that they are willing to take some ownership and responsibility to push? Do you offer them respect and show them the rewards of getting to jump on and join? Do you encourage them to join in and let them know you are going to help them?

In the end, you've empowered individuals to run around, moving and pushing and offering encouragement to the others to motivate and empower them to keep the merry-go-round spinning. Now you've created one of the most powerful predictors of success. Positive momentum! The team that grabs the momentum together wins together and has the ability to overcome all manner of obstacles and achieve massive breakthroughs in performance and potential. Go out and **do more**, **be more**, and **get more**, Coach!

SCOUTING REPORT LESSONS

▶ "Momentum is a leader's best friend."
▶ Building momentum early is difficult, but …

▶ Momentum creates breakthrough with compounding results on your investment.

▶ The GET MOR^{3}EE formula is a continuous cycle to empower people.

▶ Encouragement is the fuel that leads to empowerment.

▶ The product of reaching empowerment in the GET MOR^{3}EE formula is increased momentum.

▶ Success breeds interest.

CHAPTER TWELVE
BEWARE OF THE OTHER TWO E'S: EGO AND ENTITLEMENT

This section is like a warning label that is listed after the main ingredients of a product or after the instructions of a recipe when mixing things together. With the right ingredients, you create the perfect recipe. Leave out an ingredient like yeast when you are baking, and your bread won't rise. The right combination of ingredients can be used to create vaccines, but leave one or two ingredients out and you have a disease.

The label on the GET MOR^{3}EE formula warns us to beware of not including all the ingredients listed in the previous chapters. Failing to follow the recipe and include all the ingredients may create a nasty byproduct of **ego** and **entitlement** in our players instead of the **empowerment** we were seeking.

If we aren't consistent as leaders with our encouragement practices, then we risk a person's ego, or our own ego, becoming a replacement for the lack of encouragement. Without the consistent encouragement factor, a player on your team is left to fill that void with his or her own voice and **ego**. As a coach, we may think we're really good at recruiting people and recognizing talent, and we pat ourselves on the back for this. The mistake made many times is that we think the highly self-sufficient producers don't need our encouragement. We end up spending more time with the people who seek us out the most or we think "need" us the most. Some of us have a voice that is very strong and encouraging. Give players direction and some resources, and they will flourish. They will run full steam ahead under their own fuel and self-encouragement for some time and be highly productive. But without your recognition and encouragement they will reach a point where they feel forgotten. They still need the encouragement of the coach and to know that it's okay for them to run after their goals.

We need to remind them that "You have the support of the team, so don't worry about tripping or falling. Go, run! We want you to run, and if you fall, we will help you get back up, dust you off, help you assess why you may have tripped, and then tell you to go run again. You aren't forgotten. You aren't isolated. You aren't in this alone." If we don't reinforce the highly productive player, then ego replaces the lack of encouragement. "I" becomes a very prevalent word in their vocabulary. "I score all the goals. I catch all the passes. I'm the reason we win. I'm not getting the ball enough."

Some Christians associate ego with "edging God out," which is a strong warning for faith-based persons who look to God as their provider. The EGO acronym is a reminder that the Master has a master plan for you to live an amazing life. Is it possible that God's vision for your life, if you are willing to submit your own will to his, could be far greater than your own? So to edge God out is to allow our own pride and ego to become number one and then to miss out on that greater vision God has for our lives. I would say in the secular world it could stand for "edging goals out" or "edging greatness out."

In the greater vision of the organization or the team or whatever you believe the organization or team is achieving, creating, or solving in the world, when the ego of one or many individuals starts to supersede the goals because "I" is taking over, then achieving, creating, or curing the world's ills becomes harder or impossible because we edged "greatness" out.

We can be good. Good is all around, but good isn't always good enough. There is not a good enough cure for cancer. There is not a good enough solution to the world's food or water crisis. There is not a good enough solution to human trafficking. The whole premise in Jim Collins book *Good to Great* is that "good is the enemy of great." To achieve great solutions, you need a greatness of vision and a pursuit of excellence. To build great teams and develop great people you must not be neglectful as a coach in providing your people with encouragement and accountability. When you are neglectful in these practices, ego creeps in, and instead of empowerment you get entitlement. With ego and entitlement, you reverse momentum. It's like putting the brakes on because now you have uncertainty and discord in your culture.

Leave out motivation, and there is no vision. You don't know where you're going, and neither do your people. They are left to guess—all of them trying to make their own way. It's like 22 people rowing a boat with everyone rowing in different directions. Without motivation, you don't know what makes your players tick. You haven't learned their have-tos and want-tos, and they aren't sure if you care. They feel as if they are on their own, and ego seeds are planted.

Without ownership, your players place no value in the team and no value in each other. There is no equity being built within the team. The team becomes a hotbed of excuses. Ego becomes the owner.

Leave out responsibility, and the players take no initiative. They are always waiting on someone else to step up. They are afraid to make mistakes. They expect everything to be delivered to them. They become entitled.

Without respect, there is no heart. It becomes all about the individual. These players show no respect for the process, the vision, or team goals. It's all about "I." Ego is the only one this player respects.

No rewards, and players may hang around for a little bit, but eventually the entitled self kicks in and asks "What's in it for me?" The other properties, if given by you in high enough quantities, may be enough reward for them to stay engaged, but they will hardly be highly motivated.

The replacement for no encouragement is ego. Instead of producing empowered players, you will end up with entitled ones.

Be consistent with your encouragement practices. Be deliberate about moving your players from motivated to empowered, or risk ego and entitlement taking over your team.

Chapter 13
THE GET MOR³EE COACH

The following is the coach's version of the Stockdale Paradox.[41]

GET MOR³EE coaches see things as they are and are willing to confront the facts of their reality while maintaining unwavering faith that they will succeed.

I read the following quote in a Tony Robbins' blog post, "What Makes a Great Coach?" I think it frames the characteristics of great coaching and the picture of the GET MOR³EE coach so well that I share it with you here.

> What makes for a great coach? It's the ability to lead—to make things happen, maximize resources and inspire. It's the extraordinary quality that solves problems and helps the individual come to a new level of understanding of what is possible. And it's the skill and talent to influence and guide others to make real breakthroughs and create lasting change.
>
> Great coaches see things as they are, not worse than they are. They have a firm grasp on reality, and are honest with themselves about where they stand ... Great coaches also have vision ... Great coaches also understand strategy ... It's not always about the resources available, it's knowing how to maximize resources—someone's will, energy, creativity, courage, faith and determination—to achieve goals ... A good coach wins with great players; a great coach figures out exactly how to win with whatever players he or she has.[42]

---

41. Jim Collins popularized this concept in *Good to Great*.
42. Tony Robbins, "What Makes a Great Coach?" *Tony Robbins' Blog*, accessed September 20, 2019, https://www.tonyrobbins.com/mind-meaning/what-makes-a-great-coach/.

In the chapter The GET MOR³EE Formula, I list some qualities of a GET MOR³EE coach. The list doesn't cover all of the characteristics of a great coach, but I felt the descriptions were most closely associated with the principles of the GET MOR³EE formula. I expound on these qualities a little further for the reader in this chapter. Maybe these descriptions will help you as a coach to understand your own style or to connect your relationship and role with the application of the GET MOR³EE formula to your coaching.

You might be drawn to one or more of the qualities. Whatever qualities you are most connected to are probably your strengths. My recommendation would be to lead from there in your coaching. But do not discount the qualities or descriptions that do not resonate with you as strongly. Every quality on the list is vitally important for a GET MOR³EE coach. You will naturally be able to lead from the areas where you are strong, but don't forget about the other qualities. Occasionally glancing over these qualities will guide you and give you clues to enhance your character as a coach, just as visualizing the MOR³EE acronym will help you recall the properties of the GET MOR³EE formula in your everyday coaching.

If there are areas in the list where you feel like you are weak, which there probably will be, then be purposeful about growing in those areas and adding assistant coaches that can help complement you in those areas. Seek mentorship from other coaches who you believe display strength in the areas where you feel you are weak. If you are unsure which qualities are your strongest attributes, ask other coaches that have coached with you or seen you coach. Ask past players you've coached, and listen to the stories they recall. There are a lot of clues in the stories they repeat and share.

I am well aware that parts of the descriptions sound idyllic. What are we as leaders, visionaries, and coaches if we can't imagine an environment of excellence and opportunity for our athletes?

Before we dive into the following list, I want to encourage you. Regardless of this formula, the list of qualities, or who, where, and what level you coach ... **you are a difference maker**! You may not see it now, you may never ever know, but I **promise you**, you are positively impacting someone's life for the better right now in your coaching. You may never hear it, and your players may never have the opportunity to tell you, so I'll say it now for them.

Thank you, Coach!

THE QUALITIES OF A GET MOR³EE COACH

A GET MOR³EE coach

- *is highly people-oriented and highly results-oriented.*
- is a give-more coach. A GET MOR³EE coach loves to win.
- is a coach who cares. A GET MOR³EE coach is a leader.
- seeks knowledge. A GET MOR³EE coach pursues excellence.
- is an instiller. A GET MOR³EE coach is an enlarger.
- is a maximizer. A GET MOR³EE coach is inspirational.
- is a planner. A GET MOR³EE coach is visionary.
- is a problem solver. A GET MOR³EE coach is a championship coach.
- *sees things as they are, while maintaining unwavering faith that they will succeed.*

A GET MOR³EE Coach Is a Give-More Coach

There is not really any order to how I list the qualities of a GET MOR³EE coach, except for a **give-more** coach. The first and most valuable gift from coaches is their time. This "give more" quality is the foundation for all the other qualities. Without the investment of time by the coach, none of the other qualities exist. And I'm not referring to just the **volume** of time but also the **quality** of the time.

As you read earlier, *"power comes from the vision, not the volume."* The quality of the time in coaching I'm referring to is the purposeful, focused, and committed time to the delivery of all the other qualities with your players and teams. And it's not just about time. A GET MOR³EE coach gives more of himself. The **give-more** coach stands in the huddle with his players. The coach is on the field with the team. The relationship with the coach is intimate. In season, it's daily. The time is planned and scheduled. It's relational, and the time spent is meaningful and purposeful. The coach is always coaching and loves to see the players doing well and improving because then it means everyone has a greater chance of doing well and winning.

This coach stands shoulder to shoulder with you. She puts her arm around you. He grabs you by your face mask and lets you have it when you aren't living up to your potential. The **give-more** coach runs with you, sweats with you, stands in the rain with you, cries with you, and cheers for you. A **give-more** coach is the ultimate encourager and has the ultimate ability to tap into what motivates you and empowers you to get more. A GET MOR³EE coach gives more to get more.

A GET MOR³EE Coach Loves to Win

"I hate losing more than I want to win." (Billy Beane)

I don't know why, but I just love the movie *Moneyball.* Brad Pitt delivers this Billy Beane quote in the movie, and while no one laughs—and I don't think it's meant to be funny—I find it hilarious because it can be so true.

As a player, I think that was a very true statement for me. Especially during the regular season of games. I hated losing. In practice, I loved winning. Beating my teammates was empowering, and in doing so, I was making a statement to my teammates and myself. I belonged. And I didn't mind losing to them occasionally. I was okay with their success because we were on the same team. It just pushed me to get better. But I hated losing games to other teams. There were times when I just couldn't stop thinking about it. Mostly, I think, because I always felt I could have performed better or didn't deserve to lose. There were two times when I got beat on a play as a defensive back in high school football, and it still eats me up—and it's been 25 years!

Something changed, though, when it came to playoffs. When advancement or elimination was on the line or at that final game, I **loved** to win more than I cared about losing. There was something about the thrill of accomplishing something with my teammates after countless hours of hard work and commitment that I just loved. And that's how I am as a coach.

I love winning! And actually, this sounds strange to admit, but I love losing. What?! I love winning with my teams so much that I welcome the losses we experience at times. I may not like it, but I receive it as a gift because it shows me the areas where we need improvement that I maybe overlooked or couldn't see. And I love that.

As a GET MOR³EE coach, with the ultimate desire to get more out of my players' talent and potential, I need losses and failures for feedback so

I can create more wins when it truly matters. I love winning with people. I love sharing the experiences of winning the big games. The thought of winning on my own would never be as rewarding as having people to share the victory with.

I'm not just referring to games. I love sharing in the wins of my players. I enjoy seeing them grow and experience individual victories. I love to see the wins they accomplish outside of sport. I love to see the wins in their player development. I love to see the wins in their character development. I love to see their wins as people. Any losses they experience aren't failures; they're just opportunities for growth.

GET MOR³EE coaches love to win more than they hate to lose.

A GET MOR³EE Coach Is a Coach who Cares; A GET MOR³EE Coach Is a Leader

I included these two qualities together here because I think they are intertwined in how I view leadership. I see leadership mostly as servant leadership. Leaders care about their people. Coaches care about their players. Coaches care enough to lead their players.

I think this quote attributed to Theodore Roosevelt, the 26th president of the United States of America and the leader of the famous "Rough Riders" cavalry unit from the Spanish-American War, covers both of these qualities accurately: *"Nobody cares how much you know until they know how much you care."*

I was a history major as an undergrad, so bear with me as I share a brief history lesson. I believe it is a valuable example of leadership for your coaching.

The Rough Riders were actually the United States' first **volunteer** cavalry regiment. Colonel Roosevelt, as he was known during this time period, most likely gained some significant insight from leading this volunteer army regiment. Teddy Roosevelt wasn't famous or a household name at this time. The Rough Riders were sent to Cuba in the summer of 1898 along with another contingent of US Army regulars. The following is an excerpt of the actions of Roosevelt during the Battle of San Juan Heights.

At the start of July of 1898, the Rough Riders were under the command of Colonel Theodore Roosevelt. He had already achieved a respectable military and political career—at the start of the war of 1898 he was assistant secretary to the navy, but he resigned this job to fight on the ground in Cuba. Theodore was in his fortieth year, a bespectacled man with piercing, thoughtful eyes.

He cared deeply about his men and bitterly regretted the fact that, due to inadequate transportation from the States, they had been forced to leave not only their horses but a full third of their strength of men behind. Roosevelt's specialist cavalry regiment was forced to fight on foot.

By the time they faced Kettle Hill at San Juan Heights they were reduced to a force less than five hundred strong. Standing with the Rough Riders were the 3rd and the 10th cavalry regiments, who were also obliged to fight as foot infantry in the campaign. They were in no better condition. They were also steadily losing men both to enemy fire and to the intense heat. If action was not taken soon it would no longer be possible to take the hill.

Roosevelt took charge of the situation. After repeated requests, the regiments received the orders they had been waiting for, and they began a slow, creeping advance up the hill. They returned fire toward the Spanish positions, but ineffectively. Theodore could see disaster approaching. It was plain to him that the only way the hill might be taken was in a fast, full frontal assault.

He was mounted on his great grey mare, Texas, and rode back to speak hurriedly with the platoon captain, whose job it was to enforce Colonel Shafter's orders. Theodore urged for the charge. The captain hesitated. Theodore, recognising himself as the highest ranking officer nearby, took command. His horse's hooves thundered and kicked up clods of mud and grass as he tore back toward the front of the line. He waved his hat in the air and gave a yell, and the cry was taken up by the men around him. They stood and began to run, dashing up the slope …

On Kettle hill, Theodore Roosevelt rode back and forth along the line of his charging men, yelling encouragement to them. The rifle fire from the Spanish position had become intense, and more and more men were falling. Suddenly, the air was filled with a sound like a hundred heavy hammers. It was the Gatlings.

Roosevelt cried out to his men, who had faltered for a moment, thinking that the noise was that of Spanish machine guns.

"It's our Gatlings, men!" he shouted, "Our Gatlings!"

The cry was taken up by the Rough Riders, and by the 3rd and the 10th cavalry. Men from all three regiments had become mixed together and charged up the hill side by side. The suppressing fire from the Gatling gun battery raked back and forth across the Spanish positions on both hills. The Spanish rifle fire dwindled, replaced by screams and yells of panic.[43]

Underequipped, outmanned, and at a strategic disadvantage, Teddy Roosevelt called out for the charge of his Rough Riders, and they charged out with him. The volunteer army regiment and colonel were the first to charge up the hill, and in doing so they rallied the other members of the regular army to engage and follow with them and win the battle. All because a leader cared enough about his men to not let them remain stagnate trying to avoid losses and had the courage to lead his people boldly even without knowing the outcome.

As a coach, do I display that level of concern for the people under my care? Will I take up the charge and continually ride alongside my players, encouraging them to victory, or will I allow them to sit idly by, trying to avoid losses? Do I have the courage to lead boldly even though I don't know what the outcome will be?

A GET MOR³EE coach is a coach who cares. A GET MOR³EE coach cares enough to lead.

A GET MOR³EE Coach Seeks Knowledge

"Leadership and learning are indispensable to each other." (John F. Kennedy)[44]

This quote is attributed to the 35th president of the United States even though he never uttered those words. He may have not even written

---

43. Jack Knight, "Teddy Roosevelt Leads the Charge of the Rough Riders at the Battle of San Juan Heights," *War History Online*, February 11, 2018, https://www.warhistoryonline.com/history/teddy-roosevelt-leads-the-charge.html.

44. John F. Kennedy, "Remarks Prepared for Delivery at the Trade Mart in Dallas, TX, November 22, 1963 [Undelivered], "November 22, 1963, https://www.jfklibrary.org/archives/other-resources/john-f-kennedy-speeches/dallas-tx-trade-mart-undelivered-19631122.

them. This line was part of a speech he was to give on the day of his assassination in 1963. I think that fact is what makes this quote even more profound. Even though the words were never read aloud by JFK, the truth of them inspired people to quote him ever since.

It generally seems that all great leaders and coaches are also lifelong learners. They are students of life, leadership, and the game they coach. Many are also professors and teachers. When you ask them what they are reading, many times it is a history book. When you ask them what leaders they admire, the leaders they name might be athletic coaches but may also include business leaders, statesman, or ordinary people facing extraordinary circumstances.

GET MOR³EE coaches study their players. They study the opposition. They study other coaches. They study other sports or fields of competition, seeking knowledge that can help them get more for their athletes.

The GET MOR³EE coach is looking for any information that can help her motivate and encourage her players. She is looking for any bit of knowledge that will give her an edge in leading her players to victory on and off the field.

In the Old Testament book First Kings, there is a historical account of King Solomon, often declared as the wisest man who ever lived. In this account, it is said that God appeared to Solomon in a dream and said, "What do you want? Ask, and I will give it to you!" (1 Kgs 3:5, NLT). Solomon could have asked for anything, but this is how he responded: "Give me an understanding heart so that I can govern your people well and know the difference between right and wrong" (1 Kgs 3:9 NLT).

The GET MOR³EE coach seeks knowledge for understanding—knowledge to help gain greater understanding of the players and their opposition and understanding for how to guide the players in any circumstance. And all this driven by the motivation to **get more**.

"Any fool can know. The point is to understand." (Attributed to Albert Einstein)

A GET MOR³EE coach seeks knowledge.

A GET MOR³EE Coach Pursues Excellence

"What keeps me going is not winning, but the quest for reaching potential in myself as a coach and my kids as divers. It's the pursuit of excellence." (Attributed to Ron O'Brien, former US diving coach responsible for 12 gold medals)

I'm not sure if full excellence can ever be fully maintained. The pursuit of it can be. Earlier in this book, I discuss having a standard of excellence. A GET MOR³EE coach understands that the only true path to excellence is the pursuit of excellence. There can be no excellence in the pursuit of average. Even the pursuit of a championship may not produce excellence, but a GET MOR³EE coach understands that the pursuit of excellence may produce a championship.

A GET MOR³EE Coach Is an Instiller

GET MOR³EE coaches plant seeds. They fill their players' hearts and heads with grandiose ideas.

When I took over The King's Academy boys' soccer program, the first idea I planted in the players was that our goal was to win the state championship. That would always be our goal, and I was going to train them and treat them as a team that could accomplish that goal. For almost all of them, their highest vision for themselves was just making it through the first round of the district playoffs. We didn't win the state championship that season, but in the regular season we did defeat the team that won it the next year. Defeating this other team was something our program had never accomplished. We advanced to the district final that season. We had the most players out of any other school to receive All-County recognition. We had two players invited to play in the All-State game and one United Soccer Coaches All-American out of a group of players that didn't even consider those awards to be opportunities available to themselves. The next two seasons we advanced to the district final again, and in our third season we won the district championship, also advancing past the first round of the regional state playoff series. We again dominated the All-County awards by number of players and also had one of our players recognized as the Palm Beach Post Boys' Soccer Player of the Year. He was also named to the United Soccer Coaches All-State Team. It took time, and I don't say these things as braggadocio but just to show that all the accomplishments began with instilling an idea of who they could be. I don't believe we would have seen these results without it.

A GET MOR³EE COACH Is an Enlarger

In the **Law of Belief as Encouragement** from the chapter on encouragement in the GET MOR³EE formula, I explain the power of a coach's belief in empowering the players' belief level.

If an instiller plants the seed, then an enlarger waters the seed.

An enlarger expands the vision and beliefs of people. A coach who is an enlarger doesn't just help the players see beyond their limits; he or she removes the limits the players see. Such coaches push back the boundaries of a player's belief and enlarge the playing field literally and figuratively. Literally, in that the athletic playing field expands. What was once a tight window for a quarterback to thread a pass through becomes the sky. What looked to the free throw shooter as a tiny basket expands to a hundred-gallon bucket in the shooter's mind. What once was a tiny hole for the golfer opens up into a giant crater when putting. Figuratively, how individuals see themselves and their opportunities in life expands with the influence of an enlarger in their life. They view the world with more confidence and certainty.

A player's belief, confidence, strengths, and opportunities are greater with a GET MOR³EE coach as an enlarger.

A GET MOR³EE Coach Is a Maximizer

I gotta be honest. This quality is one of my favorites. I love to see the players I coach have success. I love to see them perform with excellence. I find great joy in helping them discover their strengths and maximize those talents. As a youth coach, it can be very tedious to repetitively teach basic skills to a player in an effort to help overcome a weakness. Helping a player discover and maximize a talent or strength that gives the individual a unique advantage over others can be exhilarating. Let's face it. The most enthusiastic response received when a player repeats a basic skill over and over sufficiently is "Good job." That is how it's supposed to be done. When a player displays proficiency in an area of gifting, the response is usually "That was amazing!"

I find it fun, challenging, and more rewarding piecing together the strengths of my players within the team. I prefer having more players running around playing and competing in their gifting. As a GET MOR³EE coach, I believe it to be my duty as a maximizer to get more out of my players' talent and potential.

A GET MOR³EE Coach Is Inspirational

We start with motivation in the GET MOR³EE formula because one of the main qualities of a successful coach is the ability to inspire players. Inspiration comes in many forms.

Inspiration may come less from what you say and more from what you do. The example you set as a coach, your preparation, work ethic, and consistency, will inspire your players to those things. Your boldness, courage, and beliefs will inspire your players' boldness, courage, and belief. Your commitment to winning will encourage your players' commitment to winning. Your modeling of respect will influence your players' display of respect.

Don't just spout inspiration. Be inspirational.

A GET MOR³EE Coach Is a Planner

"A goal without a plan is just a wish." (Attributed to Antoine de Saint-Exupéry)

A GET MOR³EE coach doesn't just assume that things will happen by accident. A GET MOR³EE coach focuses on the team's preparation more than the results, which means GET MOR³EE coaches are planners. They look to the last possible game of the season, then set goals and formulate a plan to get there.

Jack Nicklaus, a professional golf legend and winner of more major championships that any other player in the history of the game, has a legendary strategy when he approaches the tee on a new hole. Where most of us look out to the fairway, pull our driver, and think about how far we can hit, Jack Nicklaus imagines the hole first. He says he pictures the spot on the green that would give him the greatest opportunity to make a putt. Next he decides what spot in the fairway would give him the best distance and angle for reaching the location he desires on the green. Only then does he determine the best club to tee off with and pull it from his bag.

Coaches, are you planning properly for your season? Are you making preparations to have the proper equipment and time needed to run an impactful training session? Are you planning your practice sessions to make the most of the time and energy of your players? Are you creating your practice plans with the mindset of executing your game strategy? Or are you just showing up at the start of the season and every day when practice starts and just stepping up to the tee and winging it?

"By failing to prepare, you are preparing to fail." (Attributed to Benjamin Franklin)

A GET MOR³EE coach is a planner.

A GET MOR³EE COACH Is Visionary

A visionary is a person who thinks about or plans the future with imagination or wisdom. Visionaries often exhibit foresight, and their ideas may be characterized as fanciful or sometimes unpractical.

I love it. To me, a coach who is visionary thinks about the future with imagination, wisdom, and foresight. You wouldn't be a visionary if you only thought about and pursued things as they are. That wouldn't take much planning or be very inspirational. There would be no great need to instill and enlarge bold ideas and beliefs in your players and no need to maximize their talents and potential. There would be no desire for the pursuit of knowledge or excellence. The status quo doesn't call you to give more and care more. There is no great victory to pursue without a great vision and a great visionary leader to help you see it.

A GET MOR³EE Coach Is a Problem Solver

"Most people spend more time and energy going around problems than in trying to solve them." (Attributed to Henry Ford)

A GET MOR³EE coach is solution-oriented. Over the course of a season, we face numerous different challenges, some of them problems. Challenges are different than problems. Challenges are to be expected and even welcomed. Problems are usually unexpected and certainly not welcome. A GET MOR³EE coach understands the difference and recognizes when a problem has arrived.

The GET MOR³EE coach addresses problems quickly. The coach won't allow problems to fester, as problems that fester too long eventually become an infection. An infection if untreated can kill a team. A GET

MOR³EE coach is purposeful in attacking the problem and not the person. This coach seeks solutions while maintaining respect for the individuals. GET MOR³EE coaches don't avoid problems; they face them.

A GET MOR³EE coach sees things as they are while maintaining unwavering faith that the team will succeed.

A GET MOR³EE Coach Is a Championship Coach

"Champions are made from something they have deep inside of them—a desire, a dream, a vision." (Attributed to Mahatma Gandhi)

There is a desire within me as a coach to help my players achieve more. A dream of a championship, if only ever a dream. A vision of excellence.

A championship does not make a championship coach. The champion already dwells inside. A championship coach inspires others to be champions.

I'll leave you with one more fun *Moneyball* quote. Billy Beane is having a conversation with his boss, discussing the next season. You can watch the movie for the context, but the line is this: "This is why I'm here. This is why you hired me. And I've got to ask you what are we doing here … if it's not to win a championship?" Brad Pitt's character raises his hand up over his head, setting a bar. "That's my bar … My bar is to take this team to the championship."[45]

Do you want to win championship trophies that sit on a shelf or create champions that walk out into the world and create more champions that do more, be more, and get more out of their talents and potential and make a positive impact on the world?

45. *Moneyball*, directed by Bennet Miller, written by Steven Zaillian, Aaron Sorkin, Stan Chervin, and Michael Lewis (Columbia Pictures, 2011).

CHAPTER 14
THE LEGACY OF A GET MOR³EE COACH

The most influential people in my life have all been coaches. I had a front row seat to observing one of the greatest coaches of all time, my grandfather, still coaching people 30 to 40 years after he coached his last football game. I witnessed how the influence of the coach on his players was still ingrained in them 40 years after they played their last game for him. I knew what legacy was before I ever heard the word "legacy" uttered. I was experiencing it and a party to my grandfather's coaching legacy.

My grandfather was a short stocky man, strong, with calves like tree trunks and forearms like Popeye. He always seemed to be the shortest man in the room, but everyone looked at him as if he were a giant. It's an interesting thing to experience and witness when everyone in the room is looking up to the shortest man in it. His eyes and actions showed compassion for his fellow man, and there was a quiet inner strength to him. It seemed to me as if everyone knew him and everyone loved him and everyone was always excited to see him.

A COACH'S LEGACY

In 1964, my grandfather was awarded the Meritorious Service Award by the Florida Athletic Coaches Association, for "coaches who have served the high school athletic coaching profession above and beyond the call of duty."[46] In 1979 he was elected into the FACA Hall of Fame.

He was inducted into four halls of fame, as a football player and as a coach, and I was fortunate enough to be present for three of his induction ceremonies. In 1991 he was inducted into the Florida High

---

46. Award winners are listed at http://www.floridacoaches.org/meritorious-service-award.html.

School Activities Association Hall of Fame as a part of the charter class. A couple of years later, he was inducted into the Oglethorpe University Athletics Hall of Fame, his college alma mater in Atlanta, Georgia, and the St. Lucie County Sports Hall of Fame. One of my most prized possessions is his FHSAA/FACA Hall of Fame ring. It's the ring I remember him wearing the most. I love it because I can see the scratches on the stone from when he used to wear it and the turtle wax still stuck in the engravings.

I came across an article online when I was researching some of my grandfather's history. It was titled "All-time all-area football team: Who's the head coach?" and written in 2018.[47] My grandfather was nominated as one of the coaches. I include an excerpt here:

> The Treasure Coast has been home to sound outstanding football players and coaches, but who are the best of the best? ... And the nominees are ... Larry "Hunk" Slay (Ft. Pierce/Dan McCarty High 1946–1961): One of the most beloved coaches in area history, Slay played for the Eagles in the 1930s and returned as head coach in 1946 after a three-year stint as coach of Swainsboro (Georgia) and a hitch in the United States Army during World War II. His 16-year run included 99 wins—still the most in St. Lucie County history—and five Suncoast Conference championships. He later served as athletic director and St. Lucie County's athletic coordinator. Was inducted into the Florida Athletic Coaches Association Hall of Fame in 1979 and was a member of the inaugural FHSAA Hall of Fame class in 1991.

As an aside, the FHSAA bio lists him with 100 wins, so just saying! It was honestly super cool to see that 57 years after he coached his last football game, people in the local media are still writing about his coaching career.

My grandfather never coached beyond high school football. Yet he obviously had a successful career. He had one really successful undefeated team that I don't think gave up a touchdown the whole season, running a

47. Dennis Jacob, "All-time all-area football team: Who's the head coach?" *Treasure Coast Newspapers* (August 10, 2018), https://www.tcpalm.com/story/sports/high-school/football/2018/08/10/all-time-all-area-football-team-whos-head-coach/959308002/.

9–3 defense. I don't even know how you do that, but it doesn't even matter and it doesn't even matter that they were undefeated.

What matters, what I noticed as a boy, was that 30 to 40 years later I would see week after week these boys whom my grandfather coached who were now men, some of them 50-plus years old and maybe grandfathers themselves, returning to my grandfather's kitchen table–a little round wooden table with four chairs with flat wood armrests that rounded at the hands. And my grandfather would smoke a cigar every once in a while, and we'd draw up football plays, and my grandmother would bring in lunch. And if you knew my grandparents you never came to the front door; you always came around to the back door because you knew you would usually find my grandfather either out in the backyard raking leaves—he was always raking leaves, 'cause they had this massive oak tree—or sitting in the back Florida room. It had a wooden door with a jalousie window cutout in the middle with a metal frame over the glass to protect it so when you knocked it had a distinct sound that kinda rattled the glass and metal too. So they'd come to the back door and rattle it or find my grandfather in the yard, and hardly anyone called—they just dropped by to visit with Grandfather, and he received them. Nobody does that anymore—"the drop by."

So my grandfather always sat at the same chair with his back to that door, and if I was there I usually sat to his right, and his guests would either sit across from him or pull up close to his left. He lost some of the hearing in his right ear from manning a heavy machine gun in WWII. Some of these men were in athletics administration, so I might hear them receiving some advice regarding whatever situation they might be dealing with. I think sometimes they just came to check in and catch up with the old coach. I think sometimes they just needed to feel that someone still believed in them and to get a little motivation. Some of them just wanted to thank him for believing in them 40 years earlier and being another father figure to them and being willing to try to get more out of them.

And so it was by my grandfather's side that I first learned about **legacy**. No one had to tell me about it. When I first heard the word, I saw it and understood it because I had witnessed it in those little kitchen table visits. And I experienced it when inevitably one of my coaches would say to me, "Ya know, your grandfather coached me in high school." Or one of my friends' dads would say, "You're Coach Slay's grandson? I played for your grandfather in high school." Or my dad might say, "You know, so and so and so and so and so played for Papa." There were several of those.

I've heard it said that there is a difference between leadership that works and leadership that endures. My grandfather's coaching was enduring.

A COACH'S INFLUENCE

My defensive backs coach for our varsity football team in high school once said to me, "Ya know, your grandfather gave me my first PE teacher job when I graduated college." (My grandfather eventually became the athletic director for the county, twice.) And my coach began to tell a story that went something like this:

> One day, I was out at the field and I had these little kids lined up doing calisthenics, and your grandfather's office was in a building close by, and he walked out to the field behind the kids and motioned me to come over to visit with him. I made my way over to him, and he put his arm around me and turned me around, and now the kids were turned around facing us, and he said, "If anyone needs to face into the sun, let it just be you." I looked and could now see all these kids looking at me, not squinting or putting their heads down to avoid the sun, and your grandfather said, "When the kids are looking at you, they are here [hand down by waist] and you are here [hand up by face], so they end up looking straight into the sun. You're looking down, and it's better to have one person looking into the sun than twenty." And then he left me to it and went back inside.

It was a mind-opening experience for my coach, and he appreciated that my grandfather, who was the athletics administrator for the entire county, would take the time to not just tell him in passing or send him a note but spend a moment with him to show him. Today I do the same thing. If I notice I've got kids looking into the sun, I move myself or I look to set up drills so they won't be looking into the sun if I can help it. My grandfather never told me that. He never taught me that lesson directly. A coach whom he took the time to teach that lesson to, who eventually became my coach, told me a story that originated from another coach, who happened to be my grandfather, and taught me that lesson.

So as coaches, when you take the time to put your arm around someone and invest into them, it does pay returns because you may be coaching the people who will one day be coaching your grandchildren.

I remember the day my grandfather died. I was in my senior year at Palm Beach Atlantic College in West Palm Beach, Florida, and had been on the road at a soccer game in Daytona Beach, Florida, at Embry Riddle. I remember thinking about my grandfather on the way up there because I happened to hear a Jimmy Buffett song called "Captain and the Kid." That was probably about the time he passed. We didn't have cell phones then, so my mom had called my apartment. When I got back to the apartment I shared with a few other guys, one of them said my mom had called, and I knew from his face it was bad. I remember going up to the house in Ft. Pierce the next day. I made my way around to the back of my grandparents' house, went up the two red concrete steps and opened the back door, stepped into the room with the wooden table and chairs, and he wasn't there, and I collapsed against the doorframe and balled for I don't know how long until my grandmother found me there. It still brings me to tears just writing about it.

THE OAK TREE

That week, two interesting things happened. My grandmother—Gran, as we grandkids called her—said a man had stopped by the house a few days before when my grandfather was outside raking the yard. Remember the massive oak tree I mentioned? It was taller than his whitewashed two-story house, with branches that stretched out probably just as wide as the house or wider. One of my first memories—I imagine I was around two years old—was of my parents holding me as we walked up into the yard. We lived directly across the street from them until I was about eight, and I remember my parents setting me down and me running up to my grandparents under that massive oak tree, like a canopy, and them both with their arms out waiting for me and then scooping me up.

It was a massive tree, and it just dumped massive buckets of leaves. I know because all of my childhood I filled garbage cans with leaves alongside him. My brother and sister and I would jump into those big piles of leaves, and we could just disappear. We used to chase golf balls out of that tree that we had hit up there—that's how thick it was.

So my grandfather was out there under the tree raking up the piles of leaves, and a man stopped on the side of the road and got out of his car and came up into the yard to speak to him. The man said, "I've been driving by here for over forty years going to work, and I was driving by the day you planted that tree and saw you planting it, and I've watched it grow now for over forty years. I've seen you out here in the yard raking the leaves, and I had to stop to tell you that." I imagine that moment and that oak tree as a picture of the many seeds my grandfather planted in the boys he coached, who grew to become deeply rooted, solid men.

A COACH'S IMPACT

The day my grandfather died, a letter had arrived in the mail. Gran didn't find it until a few days later. It was a letter from one of his former players. And it was basically a thank you letter to my grandfather for pouring into the man as a high school kid and believing in him and being another father figure to him. And he wanted to let my grandfather know how much he meant to him and how much influence my grandfather had on who he became as a man and that he loved him for it. This former player came from out of the area that week to the funeral service after my grandmother called to tell him.

I got to talk with him some. It was a very cool experience to see how much this man whom we had never met or known until that moment loved and cherished my grandfather. This former player loved the man who was just his old high school football coach for a couple of years. My grandfather never got to read the letter, but I did.

"A coach will impact more young people in a year than the average person does in a lifetime." (Billy Graham)

You see, many of the kids you have the opportunity to coach will see and spend more time with you over the course of several months than with any other person. In the thick of the season, sometimes you may have two to three hours a day of very direct, personal contact with a kid. You have game days where you might be together from 3 p.m. to 10 p.m. I remember in high school showing up in our football locker room at 8 a.m. on a Saturday for a 1 p.m. kickoff, and it would be me, usually one other player, and our coach. Teachers might see players for five hours a week. Parents, depending on their work schedule and homelife schedule, might—might—

get a good hour a day of direct contact with their child during the high school years. The parents might be there, but the kids are doing homework, and the parents are making dinner and taking care of household things. Parents might attend all their child's games, but they are there watching and not in direct interaction during the training and learning in this team environment. And so, as a coach, you are so important. You are one of the most influential people in this person's life, and, depending on your player's situation, you might be **the most** influential person and the person your player spends the most time with each day.

You see why I am passionate about this—about giving you something as a coach that has helped me create more wins with my players. To help enhance you as the coach and empower you to get more out of your players and team.

The GET MOR³EE formula defines empowerment as a person's self-confidence to take initiative in doing more, which fuels their creativity, imagination, and passion and creates even greater momentum and motivation.

MY GRANDFATHER

The following article commemorates the legacy and impact of Coach Joseph Lawrence "Hunk" Slay.[48]

> To all who know him, he is simply "Coach." To the hundreds he has coached, and the hundreds whose lives he has touched, he is simply "Coach."
>
> A graduate of Fort Pierce High School, Oglethorp[e] University, and the University of Florida, Slay has served as football coach, athletic director and athletic coordinator in Georgia and Florida. His lifetime record is 100–40–7, with five conference championships. Slay was instrumental in the development of the Florida All-Star Football Game, and coached the South team in 1956.
>
> During his tenure as a coach, Slay became active in the Florida Athletic Coaches Association and has held every elected office.

48. "Joseph Lawrence 'Hunk' Slay," Florida High School Athletic Association, accessed October 7, 2019, https://www.fhsaa.org/departments/special-programs/hall-of-fame/members/joseph-lawrence-hunk-slay.

He also served on the FHSAA Board of Directors representing the coaches association. In 1979, Slay received the Meritorious Service Award from the Florida Athletic Coaches Association as well as being inducted into the Florida Coaches Hall of Fame and was awarded a Life Membership in the Association.

During his years as coach and athletic director in St. Lucie County, he served the community as a member and officer of the St. Lucie County Recreation Board, and is still an active member. "Coach" was a driving force in the development of St. Lucie County Lawnwood Sports Complex which consists of baseball diamonds, tennis courts, fitness trail, track and Lawnwood Football Stadium, one of the finest football stadiums in Florida.

Slay retired in 1976, but was called out of retirement in 1979 to become Athletic Coordinator for the District. During this time he completed the first Athletic Policy and Procedures Handbook for St. Lucie County Schools. He was also instrumental in developing a covered play area for all of the elementary schools, which many school districts in Florida have adopted.

His philosophy has always been that "winning is awfully important, but you can't let it overshadow all other values, and that athletics and physical education must be educationally sound to be valuable."

He retired again in 1989, but continues to serve the community as a charter member of the St. Lucie County Hall of Fame Committee.

ACKNOWLEDGMENTS

When I first began the process of sharing these ideas, the first person I went to was Coach Tom Mullins. In my 23 years of knowing "Coach," as many call him, I've maybe initiated five conversations with him, but the Holy Spirit prompted me to reach out to him first, and I wasn't really sure why. As with most things with God, it would be revealed to me in a short time. You see, Pastor Tom, as I call him, has been the lead pastor of my church, Christ Fellowship, in Palm Beach Gardens, Florida, for over 30 years. He has initiated a thousand conversations with me in his teaching and preaching and has coached me in my spiritual walk for over 20 years. I wasn't even thinking about Pastor Tom as another one of the coaches who has been so influential in my life until after that visit. The longest tenure I spent with any coach was four years. Coach Mullins has been teaching and encouraging me and many others consistently for over two decades!

A couple of weeks after our meeting, my wife comes in from the garage holding one of the books Pastor Tom authored, *The Leadership Game*. It was a signed copy, and there was a sermon notecard from August 2005 marking a place in it. I started flipping through it and noticed I had underlined several sentences and quotes throughout the book. The more I flipped, the more pieces of the GET MOR³EE formula I saw. And then it hit me. The impact and influence of Coach Mullins's, Pastor Tom's, life and teachings for all these years had become so ingrained into me that they were now just flowing out of me into my book and had influenced several important pieces of the GET MOR³EE formula.

Pastor Tom has been getting more out of me since 1996 when I first came to give my life to Christ. He's motivated me. Explained how to take ownership of my broken life, take it to the cross, and give ownership of my life over to Jesus. Taught me responsibility for my daily Christian walk and how to do it. Modeled respect and love for the lost and hurting. Showed me the rewards of a life lived well for Christ Jesus. Encouraged me to serve and share the Good News of Jesus Christ with others. Empowered me to write this book and inspire and equip a new generation of coaches to **get more** out of the talent and potential of the next generation of youth through sports.

Pastor Tom, thank you for spending that half hour with me when I called. Thank you and Ms. Donna for listening to God's calling for Christ Fellowship over three decades ago and for investing so much time into me and my family.

I've had many coaches throughout my life. I mentioned a few of the most influential coaches of my youth in the book already but want to include some special acknowledgments here.

To my little league baseball coach, Louis Clanton, for teaching me respect and keeping me accountable. Thank you to you and Ms. Peggy for spending all those years with me and always teaching me. I love you both.

To my high school football coach, track coach, and one-time YMCA soccer coach, Coach V. Thanks for giving me the "kick" to get me going, giving me opportunities, and putting your arm around me and doing it again 25 years later.

To my high school soccer coach, Wayne Cross, who is no longer with us on this earth, for modeling preparation and trying to get more out of a misfit group of soccer players.

My thanks to "the boys." I've played a lot of sports in my life, but soccer was always the most fun. Thank you to my high school soccer buddies—you know who you are. Even though we weren't always good, we always made sure we played with heart.

Thank you to my college soccer teammates. You know who you are too. You all challenged me and made me better. Special thanks to the boys who have been playing with me for over 20 years! We've seen a lot. Experienced a lot. Made a lot of new friends. And we finally got that championship and then a few more nice T-shirts later. I thank you. My knees and face do not.

I've made many friends throughout my journey who have contributed to the cause and have helped and supported me. Thanks to Coach Mac at PBAU for sharing your knowledge and reintroducing me to the hill. Thank you to our athletic directors at The King's Academy, Dr. Chris Hobbs and Adam Winters, for all your support and exemplifying servant leadership. Thank you to Kelli Fogelman for keeping them in line and Tyler Hamilton for taping our boys back together so they can keep up the good fight. Ryan Johnson, thanks for rolling with me these past few seasons. You are our ambassador of the "Quan." Thanks to all the outstanding coaches at TKA for sharing your knowledge, fields, equipment, and players and always being there to encourage me. Thank you all for modeling the pursuit of excellence.

Thank you to all of the backers of the Kickstarter campaign to launch this book! To experience all the support from our friends in the community who encouraged me, listened to me, advised me and my family—I cannot thank you enough. Thank you for believing in me and this message.

Doug Avdellas, thank you for offering your friendship and being a mentor to me and giving abundantly to me and my family.

To my sister and brother, Shaunesi and Beau, I'm proud of you. To my mom and dad, thank you for giving me life, providing for us, and for never letting me quit.

To Lisa, my beautiful bride: thank you for sharing this life with me and going on this journey. Thank you for trusting Christ in this process of turning our lives upside down once again. Thank you for blessing me with three amazing children and being a great mother to them.

Most importantly, thank you to the One, Jesus Christ, who gave it all and will never let me go. Thank you for revealing to me how truly blessed and chosen I am and for meeting all my needs. You are truly the Way, the Truth, and the Life.

GET MOR³EE COACHING

Do you desire to be a coach who gets more out of your players? Are you eager to instill the qualities of a champion within your team? Are you looking to develop winning relationships with your players? Are you ready to build a program that will do more, be more, and get more?! Coach, are you ready to make the GET MOR³EE formula a part of you and to apply it to your daily coaching activities with your team?

Then let's do it together and work to unlock the hidden potential in your players! Together, let's encourage the players we coach to maximize their potential and get more out of life! Let's help create empowered people with the self-confidence to take the initiative to do more, which will fuel their creativity, imagination, and passion and create even greater momentum and motivation for pursuing excellence in our world.

A COACH'S CALL TO ACTION

Join the *GET MORE FOR COACHES* community. Connect with us in the following ways so we can continue the conversation together and fulfill the mission of equipping **one million** coaches with the power of the GET MOR³EE formula.

- Facebook, LinkedIn, and Twitter: @JobySlay
- Instagram: @therealjobyslay
- www.getmorecoach.com
- The *GET MORE FOR COACHES* YouTube VLOG
- *GET MORE FOR COACHES* Podcast

Have us join you at your organization! GET MORE COACH Inc. provides coaching and consulting services for coaches and organizations eager to invest into the development of their coaches and the players in their care. GET MORE COACH Inc.'s coaching programs provide on-site trainings, seminars, team and club consulting services, virtual webinars, and online training for your coaches.

SPEAKING ENGAGEMENTS

The *GET MORE FOR COACHES* author and chief evangelist, Joby Slay, is available to speak and make presentations to your organization and its stakeholders at your next event. Don't have an event scheduled? Let us help you create one. To make arrangements, contact us by emailing GetMore@getmorecoach.com or visiting www.getmorecoach.com.

www.ingramcontent.com/pod-product-compliance
Lightning Source LLC
Chambersburg PA
CBHW022025090426
42739CB00006BA/285